Presented to

_____

by

_____

On the Occasion of

_____

Date

_____

LAUGHTER THERAPY

A Dose of Humor for the Christian Woman's Heart

TINA KRAUSE

BARBOUR BOOKS

An Imprint of Barbour Publishing, Inc.

ISBN 1-58660-513-5

Published by Barbour Books, an imprint of Barbour
Publishing, Inc., P.O. Box 719, Uhrichsville, Ohio 44683
www.barbourbooks.com

Member of the
Evangelical Christian
Publishers Association

DEDICATION

I lovingly dedicate this book to my husband, Jim. Without him (and his acceptance of exposure) my writing material would wane and my life would lose its luster. With him I have stability, love, and laughter. He has warmed this woman's heart for many years.

TABLE OF CONTENTS

SECTION TWO:
FUNNY FRUSTRATING MOMENTS

SECTION THREE:
FUNNY WEIGHT-WATCHING MOMENTS

INTRODUCTION

Laughter is God's medicine,
the most beautiful therapy
God ever gave humanity.
ANONYMOUS

The washing machine overflows, your toddler comes down with the chicken pox, the septic system fails, and you still have a casserole to prepare and tables to decorate for the big family reunion you promised to host in your home the next day.

It's tough to smile at times like these. Most of us would rather stay in bed, pull the sheets over our heads, and refuse to budge until things got better. Yet when life's irritants bug us more than a swarm of pesky mosquitoes and troubles spread faster than cold germs, laughter is what we need the most.

The physiological benefits of laughter have been tested from the boardroom to the hospital room. Some corporations send their CEOs to seminars on humor because they have discovered a correlation between having a sense of humor and making sound business decisions. Scientists suggest that laughter reduces stress levels, lowers blood pressure, boosts the immune system, and actually releases endorphins that diminish physical pain!

Humor is heart therapy. In fact, one doctor called laughter "internal jogging," claiming that laughing one hundred times a day works the heart as much as exercising for ten minutes on a rowing machine or fifteen minutes on an exercise bike. And what woman wouldn't rather laugh than sweat?

But long before medical science heralded the benefits of laughter, God said: "A cheerful heart is good medicine" (Proverbs 17:22); "A happy heart makes the face cheerful" (Proverbs 15:13); and, "A cheerful look brings joy to the heart, and good news gives health to the bones" (Proverbs 15:30). God created laughter to lift our spirits, lighten our loads, heal our bodies, and provide a temporary reprieve from our chaotic lives.

This book was written with that in mind. Its laughter therapy is a mixture of humor and inspiration designed to revitalize your spirit and bolster your spiritual heart rate. Each chapter invites you to a brief spiritual workout to help you find laughter despite your circumstances. Begin with the Warm-Up: a Words-a-Woman-Will-Never-Say Quotation. Then the Workout: a humorous short story with a touch of inspiration. Afterward, check your Target Heart Rate Scripture verse. As an added lift, Exercises in

LAUGHTER THERAPY

Laughter—interspersed throughout the book—are anecdotes and suggestions to help you interact with others in the joy of laughter.

In my newspaper column of the past twelve years, the most humorous and heart-lifting pieces I wrote were the ones I gleaned from events in my life that were less than funny when they first occurred. Yet amid the daily mishaps, anxieties, and frustrations, I discovered Christ's abiding presence and His everlasting joy to help me through life's blunders and bad times—whether that involved a runaway vacuum cleaner (chapter 8) or a more serious, traumatic time.

Despite your station in life and whatever mishaps, mayhem, or maladies you face today, it is my prayer that this book will—in some small way—provide you with a temporary relief from your pain, a short reprieve from your chaos, and renewed hope for a better day ahead.

So join me. Curl up in a cozy chair, indulge yourself in a warm cup of tea, and begin to bolster your spirit with workouts that require no heavy weights or physical exertion. . .just laughter, giggles, and smiles.

TINA KRAUSE

One

FUNNY EYE-OPENING MOMENTS

Chapter 1
COLD BUT CONFIDENT

THE WARM-UP

Words a Woman Will Never Say: "I feel fantastic! I'm retaining water, my stomach is bloated, I have the energy of a garden slug, and in just a few more days it's time for my annual mammogram. Womanhood doesn't get much better than this!"

THE WORKOUT

I'm waiting in the doctor's office for my annual exam. Actually, I'm sitting on the edge of the examining table dressed in something that resembles a giant paper napkin. It's cold in here. In fact, it seems the air-conditioning vent is located directly above my head, which explains the frost forming on my neck.

The nurse already took my blood pressure and has escorted me to the scale located in the hallway where any passerby can see what I weigh. I asked—as I always do—if I could take off my shoes and cut my hair before stepping on the scale.

She grinned, and I grimaced as she pushed the weight indicator higher and higher. Aside from breaking into a cold sweat when I saw my real weight—which is always five pounds more than what I weigh at home—I survived.

Barely.

So I've been sitting here, just my napkin and me, for at least twenty minutes. I know the doctor will appear soon because I heard him entering the examining room next to mine, and I hear muted conversation.

I just want to get this over. Let's see, time to mentally rehearse what I want to say. (I know: I should have written my questions down.) This is nerve-racking. My palms are sweating and my toes are freezing. I think I'm getting sick. I felt fine when I arrived, but I'm certain the man in white will have to prescribe medication for me after I'm finished here.

I hear talking in the hall. Sounds like the doctor. I brace myself. Nope, he walked away. Now I'm really nervous. I'm getting a headache and I just sneezed. Great. I can't even think straight. Why am I here anyway? I've forgotten.

Fear and intimidation strike every time I visit the doctor. Most women are acquainted with these haunting emotions. Whether in a physical exam, a final exam, or on an important project, a lack of confidence thrusts us into a whirlwind of insecurity and inferiority. For no apparent reason, otherwise confident, stable women are reduced to precarious behavior as their thoughts run amok.

But when intimidation strikes and our insecurities surface, God assures us we have no reason to fear. We can rely upon Him to restore our confidence when ours evaporates in the winds of uncertainty.

Uh-oh, I hear rustling outside the examining room door. I think this is it. The door is opening. *Lord, please help me.*

"Hi, Tina. How are you?"

"Oh, fine." Hmm, suddenly I feel pretty good.

"What seems to be the problem?"

"Well to be honest, Doc, it's this paper napkin and that air-conditioning system of yours. And why must I be publicly weighed every time I walk through the door to this place?"

Oops, perhaps a smaller dose of confidence would do.

TARGET HEART RATE SCRIPTURE

"Have no fear. . . for the LORD will be your confidence and will keep your foot from being snared."
(My foot, yes, but what about my big mouth?)

PROVERBS 3:25–26

Chapter 2
THE GIDDIES

THE WARM-UP

Words a Woman Will Never Say: "What do you say we cut short our shopping spree and check out that auto show at the race car arena?"

THE WORKOUT

Single file, I followed the other choir members to the choir loft. The organ accompanied our procession, robes swaying with each step. Church was about to begin, so I put forth an effort to look my Sunday best.

But I had one problem. Before the service, another choir member and I had engaged in some lighthearted jesting. Now we had a serious case of the giddies. Everything struck a humorous chord—the pastor's slight hop to the platform, the choir director's mannerisms, and the child squirming in the front pew.

Facing the congregation, I tried to restrain my laughter as my face flushed and tears formed. Church members peered over the tops of their hymnals looking at me. For a moment I was fine until I noticed a fly land on Mrs. Baker's head. She swatted the pest; then it landed on her face. She flinched and shooed it away, but it landed again. Her eyebrows furrowed as she stared at the pest, waiting for it to take flight. When it did, she waved her hands like a flagman at an Indy 500 race.

Instantly, my shoulders shook as laughter bubbled within like a volcano about to erupt. My friend alongside of me put her hand over her mouth and stared at the floor. Meanwhile, I prayed that I could gain control.

All eyes were on the front. *Quick, think sad thoughts,* I told myself in desperation—anything to cure the giggles. But nothing worked. The minister's mispronunciation of a name set me off again as waves of unrestrained chuckles rippled from my mouth.

Finally, the worst—an unexpected snort. Eyebrows lifted with frowns of disapproval. I wanted to disappear. *How could I allow myself to get so out of control? What must everyone think? What must the pastor think? What must* God *think?*

In an instant, the giddies vanished while humiliation and embarrassment gripped me like two giant bear claws. I bowed my head, my face now flushed for a different reason.

To my relief, the pastor whisked around and

quipped, "If a merry heart works like a medicine as the Scriptures say, someone in the choir is the healthiest person in here!"

Laughter filled the sanctuary and I was comforted. My pastor's gracious lightheartedness rescued me.

Most of us go to church dressed in our Sunday clothes and Sunday smiles. We want folks to applaud our spirituality. But occasionally something occurs to expose what we really are: human.

When our human frailties break through in waves of the ridiculous, God's mercy prevails. After all, to be human isn't a sin, but to pretend we're not is really something to laugh about!

TARGET HEART RATE SCRIPTURE

"LORD, make me to know mine end, and the measure of my days. . .that I may know how frail I am." (And should I forget. . .give me a case of the giddies to keep me in check.)

PSALM 39:4 KJV

Chapter 3
UNCHECKED PERFECTIONISM?

THE WARM-UP

Words a Woman Will Never Say: "What must I do to convince you how wrong I am? I wish you'd stop taking my word for everything. I mean, let's face it, I know nothing."

THE WORKOUT

Shocked, I was totally shocked. Seven out of the ten statements that pertained to "compulsive perfectionism" applied to me.

The author of a book I was reading developed a quiz to test tendencies toward perfectionism in women. "Check the statements that pertain to you," she wrote. Answering in the affirmative to three or more questions indicated a strong bent toward perfectionist tendencies and compulsive behavior. And perfectionists, she claimed, struggle with discontentment and intolerance.

"How could that be? I scored seven out of ten!" I barked at my husband, who sat in a chair reading.

His eyes peered over the rim of his glasses, but he didn't speak.

"Well?" I probed.

"You've gotten much better," he mumbled. His words were about as soothing as swallowing a bug.

I glared at him as my voice crescendoed. "Much *better?* What do you mean *much better?*"

He grabbed the frame of his reading glasses and removed them, a sure sign of an onslaught of candidness. "What I mean is that if you had taken the test a few years ago, you would have scored all ten."

Sulking in denial, I insisted Jim take the test. He scored two. My heightened anxiety encouraged Jim to slip into his amateur psychologist mode as he offered more unsolicited insights. "You know, Tina, I think your perfectionism is the reason why you are so impatient with people who aren't exactly like you. . . ."

Like an unexpected gust of wind in the face, his assessment left me breathless. Meanwhile, an unwelcome axiom came to mind: "A perfectionist is a person who takes great pains, then passes them on to others."

My thoughts whirled. *Does that describe me? Am I intolerant of people whose personalities are opposite of mine? Do I expect too much from others? From myself? Am I particular to a fault?*

Truth is, God is perfect but the rest of us fall short,

yet He accepts us unconditionally just as we are. Strive as we may, perfectionists cannot obtain perfection; only God can. Instead, He empowers us to practice tolerance, patience, love, and compassion for people with dissimilar personalities and lifestyles from ours.

Jim went back to reading his book, but I went to prayer. The searchlight exposed characteristics I didn't like much. And I knew from experience that the first step to conquering ugly tendencies is to take them to the Lord.

In time, who knows, as I lean on God to help me tackle my compulsive perfectionist traits, I may score a mere two a few years from now. Or hey, maybe a one. No, no, better yet a big zero. Yep, I'll purge myself of any perfectionist tendencies at all. That's right, then I'll be perfect at not being a perfectionist. . . . Oops, better get back to praying.

TARGET HEART RATE SCRIPTURE

"What a God he is! How perfect in every way! All his promises prove true. . . .For who is God except our Lord? Who but he is as a rock?" (And who am I, but an intolerant perfectionist?)
PSALM 18: 30–31 TLB

Chapter 4

CATCHALL CHAMBER

THE WARM-UP

Words a Woman Will Never Say: "What a rotten day. This new dress makes me look ten pounds slimmer, my husband cleaned the house while I was at work, and the kids threatened to do their own laundry if I refused to put my feet up and relax all evening. Now I ask you, how much more can a woman take?"

THE WORKOUT

I'm staring at the interior of my car, alias the roving catchall chamber of my life. It's the holding station for junk mail (that usually slips between the seats), a crushed Kleenex box, an empty Tic-Tac container, loose coins, and numerous crumpled napkins that I use to write notes on. The glove compartment brims with some very old ketchup and salt packets, bent straws, and a few indiscriminate grease-stained receipts from all those clandestine trips to McDonald's. And there's that clothes hanger left over from the time I stopped at a gas station to change from casual clothes into something dressier on my way to a baby shower.

I'd rather eat worms than allow the inside of my house to resemble anything close to the interior of my car. But for some reason sloppiness is acceptable behavior within the four doors of my comfortable—albeit unkempt—Dodge Shadow.

Recently, I drove my friend on an errand. As she entered my catchall chamber, I unfurled apologies, tossing and jostling items out of her way with giant heaves. "Oops, sorry about that," I blathered after she, despite my efforts, snagged her nylons on the clothes hanger when she pushed aside the crumpled napkins to find a seat.

"I don't get it," she said with a puzzled expression. "Your house is so spotless, but your car. . ."

There is no logical explanation. Nor can I explain why the inside of my purse resembles a war zone while the inside of my cabinets would charm the executive editor of Better Homes and Gardens.

Human behavior seldom makes sense. I've encountered tightwads who shudder at spending a few cents for a cup of coffee but blow thousands of greenbacks on sports cars or large screen TVs. Asked to donate a few dollars to the Lord's work and they break into a cold sweat. Yet they are the first in line to buy Lotto tickets at the convenience store.

Likewise, I sometimes think I know who I am, but my actions contradict me. I guess God is the sole discerner of hearts. Which makes me wonder: Am I really sure that I possess genuine organizational and meticulous housekeeping tendencies? After all, how confident can one be whose car resembles a nomadic dumpsite?

"You know, I may be a bag lady just waiting to emerge," I said to my friend as we cruised down the street, knee high in debris.

She studied my face, expressionless.

"Did you hear me?" I probed.

"Yep, I heard you."

"Well?"

Almost missing a stop sign, I slammed on the brakes, and like a meteor shower, the pennies I stashed on the dashboard flung themselves toward her. "You might be right," she replied, dodging the spray. "Yes, I'm sure you're right."

Spiritually as well, I often have more adjustments to make than I'm willing to admit. But with God's assistance, a transformation is possible even in the most remote catchall chambers of my heart, where He alone is able to tackle the debris.

What's more—unlike some of my car's passengers—He's unafraid of what He'll find once inside.

LAUGHTER THERAPY

TARGET HEART RATE SCRIPTURE

"Only the Lord knows! He searches all hearts and examines deepest motives." (Even the hearts and motives of undercover bag ladies who drive Dodge Shadows.) JEREMIAH 17:10 TLB

Chapter 5
A TICK ENCOUNTER

THE WARM-UP

Words a Woman Will Never Say: "My dear, you are much too organized. When will you stop putting things back where they belong? I found the scissors and masking tape stored in their proper place! And, by the way, must you always subject me to your tidy dresser drawers, orderly closets, and spotless toolshed? Give me a break."

THE WORKOUT

Call me citified, but I had never seen a tick up close and personal before, let alone one clinging to the person of someone I know well. Until recently. After walking through a wooded area of the countryside, my husband and I made a startling discovery eight hours later.

"Come here a minute," my husband called to me after he showered that evening. "Is that a bug?" (He, too, is citified.)

"Oh–h–h boy, I think that's a tick," I said, staring at his belly.

Then came the dilemma. How do we remove it? I had heard of different methods before but never paid much attention. Now I wished I had listened better.

Bending over, I analyzed the blood-sucking menace closer. "I've heard they're hard to kill," I offered. An appreciation for their biological makeup and rugged constitution escaped my husband. "We've got to get it off me!" he lashed.

I darted for the medical book and looked up "Tick: How to remove."

"Says here tick bites are potentially dangerous because of the bacteria they carry and. . ."

"Get to the removal part," he growled.

Nervously, I reached for the tweezers and pulled steadily, just as the book instructed.

"Got it!" I announced, as I tapped the tweezers on the edge of the toilet seat and flushed. Relieved, we were assured that all was well.

Later that evening, we told our tick story to our son's friend.

"What did you do with it?" he inquired.

"I flushed it down the toilet."

He hesitated before responding. "I think that's okay. But you know, you're supposed to burn ticks because if you cut them in half, they'll grow new parts."

Suddenly I had visions of the tick mutating in our

sewer system, only to surface like a sea monster at an inappropriate time and. . . Understandably, our adventure prompted me to educate myself about ticks, just in case we ever had a future encounter.

Similarly, only when we are forced to deal with a situation do we form a curiosity about that particular circumstance. For instance, when life goes well, we tend to become complacent and neglect God's instructions. But when a life-altering incident occurs and we need direction, we swiftly acquire a desire to pray and search the Scriptures for solutions. Problems, like ticks, are frightening. Yet the adversities of life often prompt us to turn to God.

At the end of the day, I echoed similar words to my husband. "Maybe it's good we had the tick encounter," I said reflectively. "Now we'll know what to do next time."

"Remove and flush?" he asked with raised eyebrows.

"No, there's much more to it than that!" I snapped, as images of a resurrected tick monster troubled my mind. "I think burning is better."

Call me paranoid and citified, but I intend to follow some instructions to the letter.

TARGET HEART RATE SCRIPTURE

"It is good for me that I have been afflicted; that I might learn thy statutes." (And learn more than I wanted to know about blood-sucking bugs.) PSALM 119:71 KJV

Chapter 6
EMBARRASSING MOMENTS

THE WARM-UP

Words a Woman Will Never Say: "Steady now. Just hand me the nail gun and shingles and I'll have this roof replaced in no time."

THE WORKOUT

Embarrassing moments follow me like baby ducks trailing their mother. Like the time I was running late so I slipped a jacket over my nightgown to drive my sons to school. Racing home to get dressed for work, a police officer flagged me down. Making hand motions, I indicated I was unable to step out of the car for fear of violating public exposure laws. As the law enforcer approached my car, I clutched my jacket around me and slithered down into the seat, remaining outwardly calm, albeit undignified. With a smile and a nod, I pretended my "nightie" was a new line of casual wear, praying he wouldn't notice but certain that he did.

So today I had another one of those moments. I was scheduled to have x-rays taken, but—due to hormonal irregularities—I feared the unthinkable. Before proceeding with the x-rays, I decided to take one of those "home tests" just to be safe.

Buying one of those kits at my age is worse than dragging toilet tissue from one's shoe while walking down the center aisle of church. When I finally mustered the courage to go to the pharmacy, my goal was to buy the kit with as little fanfare as possible.

Aiming for discretion, I bought other items with the test, even though I didn't need them, hoping the kit would slip by the clerk unnoticed. As she scanned the items, I initiated conversation to draw attention away from the box. It worked. The visions I had of her looking at me and then eyeing the box with a curious grin failed to materialize.

I thought I was home free as I exited the store, but as the automatic door swung open an alarm resounded, complete with an automated voice instructing me to return to the checkout counter. With all eyes on me, I scurried back as the salesclerk announced loud enough for the entire line of waiting people to hear, "Oh, I'm sorry. It must be your home pregnancy test!"

The humiliation of living somewhere between kneesocks and support hose served as another reminder that the secrets I try hardest to conceal are the ones most often exposed.

Actually, my attempts to disguise the real me fail more often than a student who refuses to attend class. But I've found a solution: Face the embarrassment and go on. And (ahem) pray I never run into that salesclerk or police officer again.

TARGET HEART RATE SCRIPTURE

" 'There is nothing concealed that will not be disclosed, or hidden that will not be made known. What you have said in the dark will be heard in the daylight, and what you have whispered in the ear in the inner rooms will be proclaimed from the roofs.' " (And what I buy at the pharmacy will be announced by an automated voice.)

LUKE 12:2–3

Chapter 7
TEMPERATURE CHANGES AND ROLE REVERSALS

THE WARM-UP

Words a Woman Will Never Say: "I don't know, I just feel more feminine when I bait a hook with a slimy worm and fish for days in the hot sun without bathing. It's a woman thing."

THE WORKOUT

"It's a man thing," I surmised as I observed my husband and two teenage sons shed their coats like snakeskins whenever the thermometer slipped above thirty degrees. Much to my chagrin, they dashed to and from the car in little more than long-sleeved shirts and blue jeans.

Forget gloves. They defined the term "glove compartment" literally, because that's where they'd store those fur-lined items after they unwrapped them on Christmas Day. They followed the macho male's rule of thumb: Use gloves only to remove snow from windshield. Afterward, enter car, pull gloves off, and toss them on the floor or, if energy allows, stuff them under the seat or into the glove compartment.

Forget blankets, too. In the cold winter months of my marital youth, I'd pile the bed high with fluffy quilts and thermal blankets. Meanwhile, my husband kicked them off, leaving a thin sheet wrapped around his warm-blooded frame. While I clamored for warmth, he fanned for coolness.

So imagine my surprise when something changed. "Is it hot in here?" I uttered one evening, shedding blankets in the chill of a Midwest winter. "How about if we crack the window?"

Shivering beneath the comforter, Jim lovingly replied, "Are you crazy? I'm freezing!" The midlife role reversal entered my marriage with a flurry of flying blankets and tart remarks.

Summertime continued the transition. I must sleep with air-conditioning while a ceiling fan whirls above to circulate the cool air. Meanwhile, Jim scrambles for ways to ward off the chill. "I'm going outside for a while," he announced many evenings last summer.

"What for?" I'd probe.

He'd level a look at me. "To warm up."

Every year it gets worse. "The hotter the better," Jim boasts. Meanwhile, droplets trickle down my midlife brow. Before the hormones began to seesaw, I failed to understand how Jim was comfortable in a coatless condition in the dead of winter. Nagging seemed my only option to make him realize his error. Now we've reversed roles.

It's easy to pass judgment when you've never walked in someone else's shoes, whether those shoes entail dealing with a wayward child, experiencing financial problems, facing disappointment, illness, or an aging body. We think it won't happen to us. When it does, we suddenly understand.

Adversity is the fertile ground in which understanding grows. Perhaps that's why God allows us to experience change and adversity, because then we can relate better to people who share common experiences with us.

Yes, it happened in my marriage. When Jim asked me what I wanted for Christmas, I volleyed a timely response. "Gloves. You never know when I'll need them to wipe snow off the car."

He shivered and pulled the string to his Eskimo hood tighter. But I understand. What's more, I now share something in common with my sons. It's a macho thing. No hats and gloves for us this winter. We're tough. We're cool. Yep, the colder, the better.

"But, what happened to Dad?" they asked recently, sensing the absence of their cold-weather bonding rituals.

"He's getting old," I sighed as I peeled off my gloves and shoved them under the car seat. "By the way, guys, is it hot in here?"

TARGET HEART RATE SCRIPTURE

"The mocker seeks wisdom and finds none, but knowledge comes easily to the discerning." (And to those who understand the rigors of role reversals.)   PROVERBS 14:6

Chapter 8
OLD VACUUM CLEANERS

THE WARM-UP

Words a Woman Will Never Say: "If you really loved me, you'd stop opening doors for me, buying me flowers, and sending me cutesy cards all the time. When will you learn I am capable of doing all those things myself?"

THE WORKOUT

Some folks cleave to their old stuff, but I gravitate toward the "new and better." Therein lies the problem. So when the prong to the plug on my old vacuum cleaner snapped off, I dashed to the department store to buy a brand new machine.

On a mission to find the most technologically elite, efficient vacuum cleaner on the market, I searched for one that had it all. You know, a cleaning machine that would suck layers of dust off the windowsills in microseconds, extract cat hair from the creases of my couch, and reach down between the baseboard and carpet for pine needles from last year's Christmas tree.

After much deliberation, I chose a wide, sleek power vac, with all the attachments at my fingertips. However, it had one flaw. After I took it home and actually used it, it was equivalent to pushing a semi-trailer truck up hill. So I returned it to the store and chose another.

I was sure the lightweight version would make all my housecleaning dreams come true. (Not that I fantasize about housework, mind you.) Anticipating the vacuuming experience of my life, I plugged it in and turned it on. Instantly, it propelled forward like a race car, jetting across the floor as I hung on with both hands. I quickly ascertained that it had a mind of its own and it was letting me know from the onset which one of us was in control.

"Powerful, isn't it?" I yelled to my husband above the whir, as I followed the vacuum into the kitchen, where it helped itself to a hardy portion of a carpet runner in the walkway. Instantly, its whirring sound turned to major growls and shrieks as I frantically turned the switch off and reached in to release the rug from the vacuum's monster-like grip.

"Better try a safer area," I muttered as I headed for the family room. With the old version, I was able to vacuum next to lamp cords with no problem. Not with this hungry fella. As soon as it neared the wire, it sucked the plug right out of the socket and engaged in another feeding frenzy. I panicked and let go of the handle to release the cord; the handle—due to its advanced under-the-bed-and-difficult-places-to-reach feature—dropped to the floor, catching a chunk of drywall in its path.

Exhausted, I slid to the floor, my back against the wall (so to speak). *What should I do now?*

I'm afraid I often undermine my good sense whenever I mistakenly equate new with better. Then I suffer the consequences. Finding security in what I deem superior is unwise; after all, the old has stood the test of time.

Much like the principles in God's Word. People scramble for new ways to reach God, while there is only one way: Repent of our sins and accept God's gift of salvation through Jesus Christ.

The vacuum from the underworld that devoured most of my belongings made my life more complicated than it already was. After battling with the so-called new and better, I developed a fresh appreciation for the old. I discovered that some things you keep: God's principles, tattered robes, balding husbands, aged vacuum cleaners. These are the dependable necessities of life that seldom fail.

After I replaced the cord, my old vacuum cleaner

again worked fine. It has always worked fine. Much like the fundamental truths of the Scriptures.

And believe me, my household is a safer, more peaceful place because of it.

TARGET HEART RATE SCRIPTURE

"Abhor that which is evil; cleave to that which is good." (And deposit the new vacuum in the nearest home for wayward cleaning machines.)

ROMANS 12:9 KJV

Chapter 9
DON'T BE A DRIP

THE WARM-UP

Words a Woman Will Never Say: "Forget modern conveniences. All I need to live comfortably is a canvas knapsack, a canopy of stars overhead, and some good jogging shoes for running errands."

THE WORKOUT

Camping out in nature goes against my nature, but my husband and two sons have always loved it. I, on the other hand, realized early on that a true bond with nature is achieved only in a thirty-foot Winnebago stocked with microwave, full bath, refrigerator, and bunk beds.

The first time I accompanied my family on a camping trip immediately cured me of any pioneer instincts I had. The scent of canvas mixed with mosquito spray exasperated my feminine sensitivities, and lying on a polyethylene floor wrapped in a musty sleeping bag was about as appealing as slipping a slimy little fish down my throat whole. To the macho trio, however, it was a winning combination—"roughing it" while eating sardines packed in mustard sauce straight from the can.

From the onset my biggest complaint was that camping stripped me of my natural tendency to set up housekeeping. Geared with a broom, dustpan, doormat, citronella candle, gingham tablecloth, and floral centerpiece, I joined my husband and then two young sons in the great outdoors.

Skillfully, I engaged in my usual domestic activity, much to the chagrin of the mountain men. My sons ignored my commands to zip up the tent after entering or exiting, and my husband refused to take his shoes off inside the tent, thereby leaving trails of debris on the canvas floor.

"Mom–m–m–m, we're camping," Jimmy and Jeff whined as I catapulted to spray a swarm of flying things that entered our tarpaulin abode. Evenings were much worse. After enduring a cold shower in a moth-infested bathhouse, I returned to the campsite just as the manly trio crawled into their sleeping bags fully clothed.

"But. . .I brought your pajamas," I said.

Defeated, I tried to adjust, but the strain of appearing cheerful while swatting insects, emptying sand from my shoes, and toasting marshmallows on gritty twigs was just too much. So I began to nag.

Often, I try to control my family by trying to get them to conform to my ways. When they fail to respond, I feel I have no choice but to nag. Unfortunately, the Bible equates a nagging wife to constant dripping.

My sniveling remarks started a rainstorm in the camp until I realized how much havoc I caused when I tried to fashion my family to conform to my feminine whims. So, rather than strip my family of their need to sweat, smell, and eat slimy fish, I decided something had to give. Namely, me.

After that, when the boys camped out, I visited by day, content to return to my clean house, warm bed, and functioning hot-water, bug-free shower by night. The strategy worked well for us and it cured me of my need for constant dripping.

Moreover, I learned the hard way that if you can't stand the smoke, get away from the campfire. Unless of course, a cozy Winnebago is nearby.

TARGET HEART RATE SCRIPTURE

"A quarrelsome wife is like a constant dripping."
(All right already, I got the point. Stop nagging!)
PROVERBS 19:13

Chapter 10
FEMALE VERSUS MALE LOGIC

THE WARM-UP

Words a Woman Will Never Say: "Musical, schmusical, my husband keeps nagging me to go with him to see one. But listen, I can't justify spending hard-earned money to watch a live performance of maudlin characters singing romantic songs and romping around a stage all evening."

THE WORKOUT

Jim strolled into the room and glanced at the television while I watched the conclusion of one of my home and garden shows. I love home decorating and was intrigued with the redesign of a room that professionals achieved by rearranging furniture and home accessories.

Standing in the doorway, Jim shook his head in cynicism. "I can't believe people actually get paid for doing that."

"It takes talent," I replied, eyes glued to the set.

"Well," he continued with his bordering-on-the-ridiculous male logic, "they didn't need that in Anatevka."

I leveled a look. "You mean Anatevka of *Fiddler on the Roof* fame?"

"Yep," he answered as he eased into his recliner, poised to volley more snappy responses. "No closets needed in Anatevka; just pound a nail in the wall. And when the grass needs mowing, simply let the cow out. Now, that's my kind of life."

I tuned him out, but unfortunately he was on a roll. "Ana–tevka, Ana–tevka. . . ," he sang from the movie's musical score as he stretched out in the chair with remote control in hand.

Now when a man is both illogical and blatantly provoking, he's hard to ignore. "Okay, Tevye," I scolded. "Relinquish the recliner, abstain from air-conditioning, part with the plumbing, and trade in your SUV for a horse-drawn cart."

"Hey, sounds great," he said with a grin.

"Uh-huh, sure," I countered. "One week in those surroundings would have you crooning a more accurate tune: 'If I Were a Rich Man.' "

Simplicity sounds simple when mixed with illogical thinking. Some reminisce about living in the good old days complete with an outhouse, a wood-burning stove, and a one-room schoolhouse. I admit the stories are as inviting as the aroma of warm baked bread and hot bean soup on a cold day. Yet the hardships are buried somewhere in the warm and fuzzy scenes, making those lifestyles and places look more appealing than they really were.

Logic is in the eye of the beholder, but if we trust our human reasoning apart from the reality of God's Word, we're headed for self-deception, too. A brief reality check reminds me that as inviting as rustic living sounds, I'm the woman who hates bugs, shivers and screams at the sight of a mouse, and detests dirt tracked into my home. Frankly, I prefer a clean, decorated home that boasts modern conveniences with real closets and indoor plumbing. On the other hand, I'm afraid my aspiring frontiersman is terribly deceived.

"Come on," I taunted Jim. "Like you could really hang your polo shirt on a nail after you visit the outhouse, plow the field, and escort old Bessie from the barn to eat the front lawn?"

"You bet I could," he insisted, sprawled across his cushy recliner, still humming the chorus.

So I hummed a tune of my own.

"What song is that?" Jim asked.

" 'Miracles of Miracles,' " I sighed, as I confiscated the remote and turned off the ceiling fan.

LAUGHTER THERAPY

TARGET HEART RATE SCRIPTURE

"Do not be wise in your own eyes." (Because the consequences will have you humming an annoying tune.)   PROVERBS 3:7

An Exercise in Laughter
LAUGHTER IS CONTAGIOUS. . . .

When I visited Jamaica, I learned a lesson in laughter. At first, the people and their seemingly aggressive behavior startled me. That night, I prayed, "Lord, help me to see these people through Your eyes."

The next day, as I strolled the streets of Ocho Rios, I noticed something different. Everyone with whom I made contact smiled at me.

Puzzled yet pleased, I mentioned it to my husband. "It's no wonder," he replied with a shrug. "You've been smiling at everyone ever since we left the hotel."

God answered my prayer. He planted a warm smile on my face to share with those I had once misunderstood. And they reciprocated.

Have you ever giggled and couldn't stop? (Remember my story in chapter 2?) Others will soon join in because laughter is contagious.

Jesus said, "Give and it shall be given unto you" (Luke 6:38).

Try this exercise:

Offer a smile to individuals you meet today—the bank teller, the store clerk, the cashier, a coworker. Then share your results with a friend. This exercise may not only change you, but it might bless someone who needs to smile.

Chapter 11
TRAVELING LIGHT

THE WARM-UP

Words a Woman Will Never Say: "Hmm, let's see. I have so much to wear, it's too easy for me to choose."

THE WORKOUT

"I plan to pack light on this vacation," I assured my husband as I slipped my blouses and slacks off their hangers and folded them in neat stacks inside the suitcase.

"Sure you will," he replied with a note of skepticism.

After thirty-two years of marriage and more vacations than we could afford to take, Jim knows better. My vacation checklist resembles the combined Christmas wish list of a room full of schoolchildren.

When we flew to Jamaica for a four-day stay, I filled two suitcases and a carry-on, while Jim toted one small suitcase. Men have an innate capacity for traveling light. "Just need socks, underwear, a bathing suit, and a clean shirt," he chants with the carefree demeanor of a beach bum.

But I require all the comforts of home when I hit the vacation trail. Who knows? I might need something. That's why I like to stash an ample supply of Band-Aids, aspirins, cold medicine, and a travel-size bottle of Pepto Bismol with my snacks and sewing kit. . .just in case. While I'm fumbling through the medicine chest, gathering supplies, I fret about completing all those other tasks before leaving the house. Chores like stopping the mail and newspaper, taking the cat to Mom's, locking the windows, cleaning the house (that one puzzles Jim), and making sure the refrigerator is cleaned and emptied so that it doesn't give birth to parasitic plants while we're gone.

Truth is, it's tough for a woman to travel light. I shed unnecessary baggage about as fast as I discard cellulite. I can't help myself; preparedness is my motto. After all, who knows what shift in the weather will summon the need for sweaters and blue jeans to replace bathing suits and walking shorts? And of course shoes, which occupy an entire Pullman of their own, are my traveling staples. Reeboks for jogging (if I get around to it), sandals for casual wear, leather pumps for dress, rubber sole thongs for the beach, and at least two pair of canvas slip-ons—one white, one navy.

Jim huffed and puffed as he hauled our luggage

through the airport, and he shook his head in disgust when we repeatedly had to move all the bags from one spot to another in the ticket line. Finally his frustration turned into accusatory moans. "Traveling light, huh?"

In much the same way, we ladies often have trouble traveling light spiritually, as we tote the Pullman of bitterness. Like hungry squirrels storing acorns for the winter, we store resentment to feed unforgiveness just in case we should need to defend ourselves, keep our distance, or establish our rights.

Some of us have hauled the backpack of anxiety and fear so long that worry has become second nature. Consequently, we fret about problems that are out of our control or circumstances we're unable to change.

Jesus, however, instructs us to shed the excess baggage of sin and negative emotions that weigh us down and encumber our journey. He provides rest from the heavy load long before we arrive at our final destination. The excess attitudes we tow through life are useless and destructive. That's why God instructs us to "throw off everything that hinders and the sin that so easily entangles" (Hebrews 12:1) before we allow our burdens to ruin life's trip.

With new awareness, I promised Jim that on our next trip, I would do my best to shed the excess and pack light. I've already been thinking. . .maybe if I

forgo the travel iron, the bulky beach towels, and the first-aid supplies, I will (okay, Jim will) finally tote less baggage.

As for shedding the shoes. . .all right, I'll sacrifice the Reeboks.

TARGET HEART RATE SCRIPTURE

" 'Wear my yoke—for it fits perfectly—and let me teach you; for I am gentle and humble, and you shall find rest for your souls; for I give you only light burdens.' " (Unfortunately for my husband, I give only heavy ones.)

MATTHEW 11:29–30 TLB

Chapter 12
BLUEPRINT FANTASIES

THE WARM-UP

Words a Woman Will Never Say: "I've always wanted a home life patterned after pioneer women. Dirt floors eliminate the need for vacuuming. And modern appliances, who needs them? Give me the smell of lye soap and the feel of scraped knuckles against a washboard any day."

THE WORKOUT

You know how it goes. We started talking about building homes. Blueprint fantasies, I call them. As we sat across the dinner table from our friends, our conversation went something like this:

Me: "Listen, I know exactly what I want in our new home. I want a sitting room off the master bedroom, divided by French doors. And the attached master bathroom has to be big enough for double sinks, a hot tub, and a separate shower."

Friend Bud: "Hey, that sounds like what we want, too."

Friend Sis (glancing at Bud): "And don't forget the separate makeup area with big lighted bulbs around the mirror."

Me: "Absolutely! (I look to Jim for a nod of approval). I *must* have a makeup area."

Husband Jim: "And we'll have a sunroom attached to the master bedroom and a screened-in porch off the kitchen. Of course, the breakfast nook will face the back overlooking the pond."

Our fantasizing went on for some time, as we bantered back and forth, but after we parted company, the mental carpenter's dust settled.

"The way I see it, only one thing is missing from our plans," I said out of nowhere on the drive back home.

Jim looked at me quizzically.

"What in the world are you talking about?"

"The house."

"What house?"

"Ours. There's only one thing missing in all of the plans we discussed earlier."

"What's that?"

"Money."

Two miles of silence followed as more dust settled

and reality set in.

In the Gospel of Luke, Jesus gave some good advice to those of us who run ahead of our own good sense. He said to count the cost. Admittedly, I tend to act before I consider all the facts. Carried away with emotion, I often act, speak, or plan without much forethought. As a result, I'm forced to live with the consequences of my recklessness for a long time afterward.

"I think we need to count the cost, Jim."

"That's what I've been doing the last two miles," he informs me.

"Maybe the screened-in porch can wait."

"I agree. And the sunroom, and the makeup area, and. . ."

Sensibility surfaces momentarily. "Better yet, maybe we shouldn't talk about building at all for a while," I say.

"Talking about it is okay," Jim responds in a logical tone, "as long as we agree that any talk is just our blueprint fantasies, nothing more."

"Right. So what do you think about a two-person Jacuzzi?"

More silence. . .

Whoa, I'd better stash the blueprints until he stops counting.

TARGET HEART RATE SCRIPTURE

"But don't begin until you count the cost. For who would begin construction of a building without first getting estimates and then checking to see if he has enough money to pay the bills?" (Uh, I would, that's who.)

LUKE 14:28 TLB

Chapter 13
KITTEN OR MOUNTAIN LION?

Words a Woman Will Never Say: "When my daughter asked for a pet, I encouraged her to abandon thoughts of one that required little attention. I'd much rather own a high-maintenance mammal that would enhance the development of my housekeeping capabilities while teaching my child that caring for her pet is my job."

The Workout

Eighteen years ago we found the cat of our dreams caged with other kittens at the Humane Society. Muffin was the quiet, gentle one, a tad older than the rest. As my husband held her in his arms, I could tell it was love at first sight.

I, however, looked over the other possibilities. A more diminutive, fuzzy fur ball caught my eye. "How about this one?" I asked, placing the smaller one into Jim's free hand. The kitty swiftly squirmed out of his clutches and scratched its way up Jim's vinyl jacket, leaving claw punctures along the way.

"I think not," Jim replied, prying the anchored kitten off his shoulder. "But what about this one?" he said with a lilt to his voice.

He gazed down at Muffin with embracing eyes as our then young children stroked her yellow coat of fur. So Muffin it was. We did, after all, pray for a cat that would best suit our family, and Muffin fit the bill.

From the onset, Muffin imaged our family's personality, well suited to the tone and mood of our home. From the start, she differed from her feline counterparts. Totally dependent on us, she behaved more like a dog than a cat, except for the benefits of kitty littering, if you know what I mean. She sat up for her food (no kidding), and we trained her to stay off the good furniture. She confined herself to our laps, her favorite chair, or the foot of our bed.

But now in her golden years I've noticed a change. She's still a terrific tabby. Just different. Apart from her sagging, mangy frame and slower pace, her personality has acquired a demanding insistence.

In her youth, we seldom heard her bellow a hardy meow. Once in a while she'd open her mouth, but nothing much came out, except a faint squeak. Actually, we assumed she had no voice.

Now we know better. Muffin talks a lot these

days. For no reason at all, she appears at my feet and meows. Loudly. And repeatedly. Even if she's been fed, brushed, and stroked, she gripes. Often she just sits and stares up at me as if to announce, "Look, I'm old; if I want to complain for no reason at all I'm entitled. Haven't I been good all my life?"

Some say that pets resemble their owners in personality and sometimes in appearance (I'm in trouble if that's true). Interestingly, I've noticed one of Muffin's annoying traits developing in myself. The older I get, the more opinionated I've become. Okay, mouthy is probably a better word. "I won't put up with *that* anymore," I boast. The docile pussycat of my younger days is turning into a mountain lion.

Frankly, it's a characteristic I'd rather not have. I mean, think about it. I could live an exemplary life only to blow it later if I allow an "I'm entitled" attitude to dominate my moods and actions.

Contrary to the stereotypes, age has its benefits, but haughtiness isn't one of them. Not from God's perspective.

Did you hear that, Muffin? She just jumped atop the dryer, demanding to be brushed.

"Muffin, your insistent ways are blowing your good reputation."

"Me—ow—ow—ow!"

Hmm, I wonder if she's trying to tell me the same thing?

TARGET HEART RATE SCRIPTURE

"Love is very patient and kind. . .never boastful or proud, never haughty or selfish or rude. Love does not demand its own way." (But Muffin sure does, and if I'm not careful, I could be next.)

1 CORINTHIANS 13:4–5

Chapter 14
MEMORY LOST IN POST-ITS

THE WARM-UP

Words a Woman Will Never Say: "As I age, my memory sharpens. Lists, who needs them? My to-do list is stored like a computer file in this fantastic brain of mine."

THE WORKOUT

I read somewhere that the human brain is capable of storing two billion bits of data in a lifetime. So why does my memory fail me continually?

Familiar faces with no names taunt me to dig deep within the lost files of my memory bank. Two such smiling faces approached me at a dinner event recently. As the twosome walked toward our table, I nervously elbowed my husband, whispering, "Hurry, what're their names? I forgot."

"Susan and Ralph," he replied out of the side of his mouth.

"Ah yes, that's right," I said just in time to greet them, pretending I knew their names all the while.

A kind pastor once assured me that my memory lapses were nothing more than what he termed "a knowledge overload." That sounded good, even scholarly. So I bought it, though at times I'm sure the phrase is a euphemism for my real condition: hopelessly scatterbrained.

Like the time I climbed into bed with a book in one hand, searching for my neck-roll pillow. Moments later I discovered the pillow had been in my other hand the entire time. Earlier in the day I poured myself a glass of milk and instead of returning the milk carton to the refrigerator shelf, I placed it inside the kitchen cabinet. That was the same day I lost my driver's license. The following day had been no better. I cut off tags from a new pair of slacks and unwittingly dropped the tags into the toilet, instead of in the trash can alongside it. Mindlessly, I flushed, and then, panicked, I plunged my arm into the commode to rescue the tags before they obstructed the sewer system.

About that time Jim walked in. "I don't know what's wrong with me," I said, fishing for encouragement with soggy, drippy tags in hand. He arched his eyebrows and exited without a word.

Whatever the reason for my recurrent problem, I've learned to become an obsessive list maker. Napkins, envelopes, and check deposit slips serve as surrogate notepads on which to scribble thoughts, names, and to-do lists. In fact, I've been known to jot down thoughts, guaranteed to slip my mind seconds later, on pieces of paper the size of a postage stamp. If a paper has at least one square inch of empty space, I'll fill it.

Mindlessness is a scary phenomenon as evidenced by my habit of using sticky pieces of yellow paper. Post-its are everywhere—stuck to my refrigerator door, peering from my pocket calendar, hanging from my computer, and shoved inside my wallet. Most of the time, this method of memory file works to my advantage. Well, all right, sometimes.

Except one morning. I was making the bed, when I happened to glance at the yellow note stuck to my headboard, reminding me to get a check in the mail. Stopping, I picked up my purse and walked to the kitchen counter to write out the check.

Afterward, I noticed that the cat was licking the cabinet door where her food is stored. I quickly fed her to avoid spending the afternoon with a bottle of Murphy's Oil. Then, while still in the kitchen, I remembered to unload the dishwasher. . .until I realized that the clothes were in the dryer from the night before. I trekked downstairs to take care of that, too, while completing other chores along the way.

It didn't occur to me until hours later that my bed

was still half-made, which in turn reminded me of the half-emptied dishwasher. Unfortunately, Post-its are merely good for some things, some times.

I have, however, found a better alternative to my reliance on sticky pieces of paper. When daily chores and responsibilities shift my knowledge overload into overdrive, God cues me to remember the things listed on the pages of His Word, the Bible. One of them is to commit everything I do to the Lord, so He will establish my thoughts. Simple, effective, and really worth remembering—a sure cure for knowledge overload, absentmindedness, or just pure density.

I'm thankful that although I lose sight of many things, God remembers to care for me in my mindless state. His Word is a vital bit of data stored within my memory bank; it surfaces during the moments that I need peace and guidance the most. That's something I'm not likely to forget.

Remembering the name of that couple, however, is another story. What were their names again?

TARGET HEART RATE SCRIPTURE

"Commit thy works unto the LORD, and thy thoughts shall be established." (And should you forget, use a Post-it note.)   PROVERBS 16:3 KJV

Chapter 15
BULK IS BEAUTIFUL

THE WARM-UP

Words a Woman Will Never Say: "Less is better, especially when it comes to closet space. I tell you, I have so much room now I don't know how to fill it all."

THE WORKOUT

"This isn't working," I sighed as I shoved items to make room on our utility shelf for what we just purchased.

"Sure it will," my husband insisted, as he shifted mammoth packages of toilet paper, bath soap, and paper towels.

"But it's ugly and unsightly," I argued. "Just look at this stuff; it towers three feet in the air!"

This happens every time my husband is turned loose in the aisles of a discount store. He resembles one of those exuberant contestants on "Supermarket Sweepstakes." With great swoops he hurls giant-size boxes of tea bags, microwave popcorn, and laundry detergent into the cart as he whirls through each lane.

His explanation? "We'll save a lot of money that way and we'll never run out of what we need."

Shopping with a bulk buyer is like taking a lesson in economics from Alan Greenspan. "Look here," my husband instructs, pointing at the label, "we're getting twice the amount for a few dollars more."

While he educates me, I mentally arrange the shelves at home to make room for the volume. Our home just isn't big enough to accommodate oversized bottles of ketchup, shampoo, and other household goods. The utility room already looks like a miniature Sam's warehouse.

Nevertheless, loaded down with bulk, we return home to the task of moving, stacking, and rearranging. As soon as our makeshift warehouse shows the first signs of inventory lack, the busy buyer will again make tracks to his haven of discount delight.

Regardless of how extreme my significant other's behavior appears, it's not all that unusual. When it comes to temporal things, most of us derive pleasure and contentment from knowing our lives are stocked with plenty. Relentlessly, we store up earthly commodities as a means of security, fueling our sense of accomplishment.

But Jesus, the Master Economist, instructs us to store up our treasures in heaven instead. Long after our household supplies dwindle, our homes deteriorate, and our furnishings wear out, our eternal storehouse will last. Celestial shoppers, obedient to God's Word, stock their heavenly homes with huge quantities of faith, giant-size boxes of forgiveness, and family-size bottles of love, mercy, and compassion.

And unlike my skimpy storage room, God's storehouse holds a volume of wealth, not in unsightly stacks crammed in a basement utility room, but in chambers of gold brimming with the treasures of the rich in heart.

In God's house, bulk is beautiful. Did you hear that, Jim?

Uh-oh, he's at it again. This time we'd better make room for some celestial shopping.

TARGET HEART RATE SCRIPTURE

" 'Do not store up for yourselves treasures on earth, where moth and rust destroy. . . . But store up for yourselves treasures in heaven.' " (Where there's plenty of room for bulk buying and bulk buyers.)　　　　　　　　MATTHEW 6:19–20

Chapter 16
CARS, KIDS, AND OTHER INTERESTS

THE WARM-UP

Words a Woman Will Never Say: "I'm so tired of listening to my husband complain about my so-called obsession with cars and sports. So I decided to compromise. I'll talk recipes and home decorating with him, if he'll escort me to the next heavyweight boxing match."

THE WORKOUT

My husband notices things of little interest to me. The color and model of cars is one. As we drove into a restaurant parking lot recently, Jim observed a white Chevy Caprice. "Hey, I think the Smiths are here; that's their car," he remarked. Frankly, I wouldn't know if the Smiths drove a pickup truck or a Cadillac. Makes no difference to me. The day I recognize someone's car will be the day my husband buys designer sheets.

Perhaps the reason for my disinterest is that cars bore me. When we shop for a vehicle, the only feature that entices me is the color. Meanwhile, driving from one car dealership to another, Jim analyzes our choices.

"The Buick Regal is a six-cylinder, but twenty-six miles to the gallon is decent, and I liked the precision steering," he'll say, waiting for my reaction.

"Doesn't matter," I mutter, gazing out the side window.

"Huh? What didn't you like?" he asks, eyes flashing.

"It was white. I want bright red."

"That's it? You didn't like it because it was white?"

"No, it also had an ugly interior."

In the same way Jim associates cars with people, he also recognizes parents by their children. When our sons, Jimmy and Jeff, were growing up, Jim knew all their classmates by name, mainly due to his involvement with our kids' sporting activities. We'd walk into the gymnasium for a basketball game and he'd say hello to at least five kids before we were seated. My usual apathy and deliberate ignorance kept me from committing too many names to memory. But occasionally, my curiosity would pique and I'd ask who they were.

"Oh, that's Brad. John and Pat Brook's kid," he'd say, matter-of-factly. "You know Brad; he played Little League with Jimmy."

I'd contemplate for a moment and realize my efforts were fruitless. Observing my blank stare, he'd launch into his usual recall-that-kid-blast-from-the-past, detailing facts with precise recall. The less responsive I was, the more insistent he'd become.

"I know you know him," he'd say emphatically. "Remember the summer when Jimmy got hit by a baseball? It was the eighth inning with two outs. Little Larry Jones was on third base and—"

"Who's little Larry Jones?" I'd interrupt.

"He's Helen and Frank's boy. Anyway, Jimmy was up to bat when the ball hit him and his knee swelled like a grapefruit. Remember?" Despite my silence, he kept explaining. "Well, the kid who ran to get the ice was Brad."

Brad, Larry, Schmary, I was clueless. I loved kids, but this was ridiculous.

Most of us recall persons, places, or things that interest us. If our priority is shopping, then we know the best stores with the best buys; if it's sports, we stay abreast of our favorite teams; if it's cars, we memorize models with ease.

Spiritually, we're much the same. We internalize matters that interest us most. Our commitment to the application of God's Word is in direct proportion to our level of devotion to God. "Set your affections on things above, not on things on the earth," the Book of Colossians (KJV) says. Taking time to pray and read the Scriptures is a joy when our primary interest is to seek

God, but if our interests are strictly temporal, then we tend to ignore our spiritual well-being.

What's my primary interest? Certainly not vehicles. Of course, if the vehicle is fire-engine red and will transport me to the nearest sale, then that's a car of a different color.

TARGET HEART RATE SCRIPTURE

" 'For where your treasure is, there your heart will be also.' " (So what interests you?)

MATTHEW 6:21

Chapter 17
WHAT A HEEL

THE WARM-UP

Words a Woman Will Never Say: "They had these coffee-beige, steel-toed boots on sale, and I just had to buy them. Their color coordinates with just about everything, and boots are so practical."

THE WORKOUT

I'm rebelling. Years ago I wouldn't dream of wearing a dress without also sporting three-inch heels. Not today. With age comes wisdom, along with an aching back, sore arches, and intolerance for the absurd. Thus, I refuse to wear shoes with heels higher than two inches.

My younger years, however, were much different. I walked miles in spike heels that required the balance and coordination of a trapeze artist; I clomped along in wooden wedgies; and I strained in silence to keep my fat foot inside skimpy, backless pumps.

Once again, current fashion trends have taken a new low, or shall I say high? "Stacked heels" are in vogue. You know, those retro seventies-looking shoes that require a ladder to get into? So I ask, what's the point? A small heel is reasonable, but what women do in the name of fashion is masochistic.

"But heels make my legs look better," one young woman insisted. So does liposuction, but who wants to go through that? If I aspired to walk tiptoed, I'd take ballet lessons.

There comes a time in life when practicality wins over appearance. Loafers, flats, sandals, sneakers, even moccasins sound better all the time.

Recently I tried to give my daughter-in-law a new pair of loafers that didn't fit me. "No thanks, Mom," Theresa said. "They look like old-lady shoes."

"What?" I protested. "Look how comfortable they are. They've got all that cushioning in the insole. . . ." She shook her head and grinned. Poor girl, she's in her twenties and still has a lot of tiptoeing torture to endure before she falls off her high heels and comes down to flats.

At least my husband feels as I do. After twenty-five years of wearing suits and ties, he has rebelled, too. Somewhere between mayhem and midlife, he realized that wrapping a colorful cloth around his neck and knotting it at the Adam's apple served no constructive purpose. He no longer cares if our culture requires the well-dressed man to parade around all day bound and tied.

Don't misunderstand; proper dress serves a positive purpose. But as my polo-shirt husband aptly states it: "One can look professional and still be practical." The question is, what objective do high heels or strangulating ties serve?

Unlike cultural trends, God's Word encourages us to clothe ourselves in purposeful attire. "Put on all of God's armor so that you will be able to stand safe against all strategies and tricks of Satan. . . .Use every piece of God's armor to resist the enemy whenever he attacks, and when it is all over, you will still be standing up" (Ephesians 6:11–13 TLB).

Every item of our spiritual attire equips us to live full, victorious lives and to serve others who need to know God cares. Truth is, if we would concentrate more on our spiritual attire than we do on our physical, we could transform our world. Instead, we often conform to worldly trends and ignore God's decrees.

That's something we don't like to admit. But hey, if the shoe fits, wear it. . . . Unless, of course, the heels are higher than two inches.

LAUGHTER THERAPY

TARGET HEART RATE SCRIPTURE

"You will need the strong belt of truth and the breastplate of God's approval. Wear shoes that are able to speed you on as you preach the Good News." (And try doing that in high heels!)

EPHESIANS 6:14–15 TLB

Chapter 18
PROUD GARBAGE PICKER

THE WARM-UP

Words a Woman Will Never Say: "I live for Tupperware home parties. Even if the representative didn't offer me free merchandise, I'd host parties just for fun."

THE WORKOUT

I have a confession to make. I'm a garbage picker. Not the full-fledged type who drives through neighborhoods in a pickup truck on garbage day. I'm much more discreet than that. I pick my garbage on foot.

It's not intentional, mind you. I don't set out to rummage through my neighbors' trash; I simply observe interesting items while I pass random trash cans along my jogging route.

In fact, garbage day provides great aerobic training, because I run faster on the days I see something of value. Feverishly, I finish my course in record time, hoping no one else will notice the discarded treasure before I have time to get home, jump in my car, and head for the heap.

But there are always exceptions. Like the rainy day when I spotted a canvas chaise lounge about a mile away from my home. I tucked the chair under my arm like a surfboard and sprinted to my girlfriend's house a few blocks away. "Hey, would you keep this for me until I finish my run?" I asked, panting and dripping at her door.

My friend stared at me in disbelief. I realize now how foolish I must appear when I do such things. Like the time I wheelbarrowed two potted evergreens down the street to my home. Or the day I trotted down the road clutching almost-like-new spice racks. These items were of significant value to me, enough for me to go to any length to retrieve them from the trash.

Fortunately, God feels much the same way about us. I recall a story about a young, desperate girl who was about to give up on life. That evening, God stirred a Christian friend to pray for her in the middle of the night. Unable to sleep, the Christian woman sensed a need to contact the girl. Her concern heightened when she telephoned, but received no answer.

Concerned, the woman dressed and drove twenty miles in the middle of the night to rush to the girl's side, just in time. Compassionately, she counseled her troubled friend, reassuring her of God's love and forgiveness. That night, God plucked a young woman from the trash bin of life, and she embraced the message of the gospel. Today, she is no longer a part of life's discarded refuse, but a productive, shining jewel who rescues others from the same hopelessness she once knew.

After hearing that story, I made a decision. Only full-fledged treasure hunting will do. No, I won't roam the neighborhood in a pickup truck, searching for temporal objects of value. Instead I'll comb the corridors of castaway souls who occupy the street curbs of life each day—the true forsaken treasures.

For what's rubbish to one is riches to God. Besides, I could use a little spiritual aerobic training.

TARGET HEART RATE SCRIPTURE

Jesus said, " 'And whoever comes to me I will never drive away.' " (Not even the characters who tote chaise lounge chairs under their arms?)

JOHN 6:37

An Exercise in Laughter
LAUGHTER IS FUN. . . .

Have you noticed that children have an inherent ability to have fun? Uninhibited, they lose themselves in giggles, frivolity, and spontaneous play.

One steamy August afternoon, my then three-year-old grandson Ian helped me water the flowers. As he held the garden hose, I stood behind him to ensure he directed the force of the spray in the right direction. Briefly, I turned away to stoop down and pull a few weeds.

"Nana!" Ian shouted as he spun around and sprinkled me with the hose. Dodging the spray, I ran across the lawn, while Ian trailed behind, giggling and laughing. Hearing the ruckus, Jim appeared from the garage. Swiftly, our little jokester turned the spray on his papa, too. After I retrieved the hose from Ian's tiny grip, all three of us were running, laughing, and sprinkling each other, dripping wet.

Try this exercise:

Abandon your adult inhibitions
and do something fun and spon-
taneous. Walk barefoot in the rain (and remember to
splash in the puddles). Finger paint with a child. Picnic
at the park and take along a Frisbee. In a group, share
your uninhibited moments of frivolity and discuss the
benefits of spontaneity.

Enjoy the fun and laughter that the unexpected
brings!

Chapter 19
OFFICE JUNK ROOM

THE WARM-UP

Words a Woman Will Never Say: "Clutter gives my home a lived-in appeal like nothing else can. That's why I litter every crevasse of my home and teach my family to do the same."

THE WORKOUT

My office is the only room in the house that looks like the interior of a second-hand shop. Items that fit nowhere else end up there.

A narrow pathway—like the parting of the Red Sea—leads to my desk, flanked by my grandson's toys, his deflated swimming pool, and assorted pieces of unmatched furniture. Framed family photos clutter every conceivable space. Post-its dangle from my computer, and pens and paper clips hide beneath layers of files. The trash can overflows with crumpled paper and not a few candy wrappers (my brain food). Stacks of books tower atop one another in crooked mishap, and mounds of stuff ascend from beneath my desk. Junk mail I've not yet determined garbage worthy waits to be read. . . someday.

The only people who dare to enter my den of debris are my grandson and me. Ian sees it as a fun challenge. He squeezes his tiny body between my credenza and his basket of toys, scaling the mounds like a mountain goat.

"I don't get it," my husband mused one day, standing a safe distance at the door. "You're such a tidy person. What happened here?"

It's easier to close off the room from the rest of the house than to face the eyesore and rent a bulldozer to clear it out. But Jim's comment moved me to take notice. I had lived in denial too long; the word "office" had become a euphemism for "junk room."

So one Saturday afternoon I rolled up my sleeves to tackle the six-hour job of de-cluttering the room. With eyes squeezed shut and a slight grimace, I discarded boxes of old files, magazines, and newsletters I had kept for years. Yes, even old warranties to items I no longer own and dehydrated felt markers hit the trail. . .I mean, pail.

As I heaved bulging trash bags out the door, I considered how places of my life get messy, too. Bad habits, negative thoughts, or unpleasant moods drift into my character, paralyzing my spirit. Though every other "room" in my spiritual house appears neat and tidy, one junk thought or habit taints my entire character. Thus, my whole life is affected.

Disciplining ourselves to maintain a tidy office—or a clean heart—frees us to enjoy a higher quality of living. But it takes some effort. De-cluttering isn't for the slothful of spirit. The first step is to admit our need, ask for divine help, and then follow through.

I must admit, working in an orderly room is heavenly. I even receive visitors who actually tread beyond the doorway—perhaps because now they have room to move; or maybe it's because the environment has improved, making my office a more inviting space. Who knows?

Regardless, my junk room left the office.

TARGET HEART RATE SCRIPTURE

"Cleanse me from these hidden faults. And keep me from deliberate wrongs; help me to stop doing them. Only then can I be free." (And only then will folks feel safe to tread inside my former junk room.) PSALM 19:13 TLB

Chapter 20
FASHION AND THE VINTAGE LOOK

THE WARM-UP

Words a Woman Will Never Say: "Crow's-feet around my eyes, a sagging chin, and a wrinkled forehead give me that vintage look that's so fashionable these days."

THE WORKOUT

Browsing through a nursery, I noticed a cluster of tall purple flowers that graced the curving entrance. "How much are they?" I inquired inside.

"Oh, we can't sell those; it's against the law."

I was dumbfounded when the employee said that the plant was the same one that grows along railroad tracks and roadsides. "Guess you'll have to dig them out by the roadside," she said with a shrug.

Oh the irony of it all. Remember when clusters of wild grass were a nuisance, springing up along fence lines and between cracks in the pavement? Now we call them "ornamental grass" and they have a price tag to match. What was once deemed a weed, we covet as a worthy find today.

There was a time when transplanting weeds in our garden would make us a candidate for the funny farm. Then again, I remember a time when torn, faded jeans were worn only when working in the fields, and body piercing was a barbaric ritual performed by cannibals. Not anymore.

And let's not forget the hottest trend in furniture and home decorating. Sane, normal women sandpaper the edges of new furniture, apply coats of milky glaze, and gouge new wood surfaces to achieve the "distressed look." And for a more aged appearance, try tea-stained wallpaper.

So I began to think about the appeal of expensive weeds and aged furniture. Wouldn't it be great if the next trend promoted the distressed look for women? Fashion magazines would feature middle-aged and elderly cover girls. Teenage girls would scramble to read the latest techniques on how to achieve the sagging, wrinkled look to create a more vintage appearance. "Wrinkled is right," would resound as the modern mantra as former fashion beauties would attempt to fatten their slender bodies and sag their firmed faces. Now that's a fashion statement I'd enjoy.

Truth is, anything goes when it comes to fads.

One quote reads: "Fashion is something barbarous, for it produces innovation without reason and imitation without benefit." Trends influence entire societies—usually in an outlandish manner—while women hasten to align with the latest fads.

Some claim that Christianity and the Bible are unfashionable. New religions appeal to our whatever-feels-good mentalities while the Holy Scriptures are deemed inapplicable for today. Consequently, what was once thought sinful is now acceptable; what once brought shame is enthusiastically embraced.

Yet the Scriptures have endured the test of time and are still the most timely, powerful, and applicable source of guidance for daily living. Unlike modern thinking and awkward trends, God never changes and His Word is as relevant and fashionable today as it was thousands of years ago.

That's a worthy point to consider before I transplant purple weeds, distress my furniture, and anxiously wait for middle age to come in vogue. Some things are better left alone. As for body piercing? Let's not even go there!

LAUGHTER THERAPY

TARGET HEART RATE SCRIPTURE

"Don't let others spoil your faith and joy with their philosophies, their wrong and shallow answers built on men's thoughts and ideas." (And on silly fashion trends. . .unless the fad glorifies a woman's "vintage" look, of course.)

COLOSSIANS 2:8 TLB

Two

FUNNY FRUSTRATING MOMENTS

Chapter 21

ALL THINGS ARE POSSIBLE. . .*BANG! CRUNCH!*

THE WARM-UP

Words a Woman Will Never Say: "My idea of a perfect vacation is to awaken at 5 A.M., slip hip boots over my camouflage jumpsuit, and stand for hours in freezing water while my husband sounds duck calls to the sway of cattails dancing in the icy breeze."

THE WORKOUT

"It's only for a few days," my husband insisted. "What could happen in a few days?"

I shuddered at the possibilities. When my husband's business acquaintance offered to lend us his Winnebago for the weekend, Jim was thrilled. But I cringed. I have trouble borrowing a Band-Aid, let alone barreling down a congested highway in someone else's home on wheels.

"But just think," Jim coaxed, "it has a shower, refrigerator, and microwave." I admit, the thought of camping in luxury enticed me. For years I shunned camping in the thick of mosquito territory; I refused to sleep in a musty tent and toast marshmallows on gritty twigs. "All right," I agreed reluctantly, "but I'm uncomfortable about this."

Borrowing someone's expensive camper was bad enough, but a few days before our departure, Jim mindlessly shared our weekend plans with Bob, an obnoxious neighbor.

"Did you say the camper sleeps eight?" Bob echoed with raised eyebrows. "We're free this weekend. Mind if we come along?"

Trouble loomed from the start. Our sons—then ages ten and fourteen—were so thrilled about spending two whole days with Bob's seven-year-old child from the underworld that our oldest son pitched a tent a considerable distance away from the camper.

After listening to five hours of combative discussion between our camp guests—Bob, Judy, and their overindulged son Michael—our son's musty tent began to possess the charm of a country inn. With gritty twig in hand and my pioneer spirit revived, I was eager to downscale from cookstoves to campfires. Jim, however, insisted that I stay with the adults. "Just ignore Bob and Judy's feuds," he said with the demeanor of a professional psychologist.

So we bunked in for our first night. Though the

temperature was a comfortable seventy-five degrees, the heat kicked on about midnight. I scrambled from my bed to adjust the thermostat, but the flow of hot air pumped into our compact abode faster than flood-waters bursting through a dam. As I tapped on the thermostat and mumbled to myself, good neighbor Bob woke up and meandered to the bathroom at the back of the camper. As he reached for the handle, the bathroom door fell off its hinges.

By now everyone in the camper was awake. Some awakened to the increasingly sauna-like atmosphere. But most woke up to the sound of my husband's yelp when Bob startled him with door in hand, causing Jim to lurch forward and hit his head on the overhead bunk.

The following day was no better. The refrigerator died, forcing us to pack all its contents into a cooler. Meanwhile, a peculiar dripping at the bottom of the camper in the area of the latrine formed an offensive-smelling puddle on the ground outside.

Flies buzzed and emotions soared. By now, I sus-pected that our uninvited guests had brought a few un-invited guests of their own to haunt, taunt, and destroy our weekend. And we didn't do many fun camping activities. After all, damage repair takes time, whether on the camper or our strained marriage.

Soon the uninvited guests decided the camper

that slept eight was too much work, so they abandoned camp. Truthfully, I think the combative discussions between Jim and I became too much for them.

In the time that remained, I scrubbed down the borrowed burden to return to its owners, hopefully unscathed. "With God, all things are possible," I recited to myself, cleaving to the hope that even disastrous weekends could turn around. Besides, what more could possibly happen?

We enjoyed an entire half day of peace before packing to leave. As we exited the campsite for the open road, Jim drove the Winnebago, while the kids and I followed in our van, anxious to return the camper to its owner.

Nearing our destination, the camper approached a stop sign when. . .*bang! crunch!* The sound of steel and glass heralded my worst fears. From behind I saw the camper's windshield shatter into tiny pieces. The front end crushed like an accordion when the truck driver in front of Jim slammed on his brakes. Thankfully, everyone was okay. . .well, sort of.

Since then we borrow no more, not even a cup of sugar. Too risky. I mean, consider the possibilities. I could stumble on the way out of my neighbor's house and spill sugar all over her new carpet; or I might slip on the steps and shatter tiny pieces of the broken cup

all over her porch; or I could step on her cat and maim it for life; or knock on the door and pull the door-knocker off. Or, Bob, Judy, and Michael might show up and want to borrow sugar, too. Then what?

I shudder at the possibilities.

TARGET HEART RATE SCRIPTURE

"For the thing which I greatly feared is come upon me, and that which I was afraid of is come unto me." (After all, anything is possible if the burden we bear is borrowed.)   JOB 3:25 KJV

Chapter 22
SHORTCUTS AND GARAGE SALES

THE WARM-UP

Words a Woman Will Never Say: "Well, he did it again. While I was at work, my husband went on another cleaning frenzy and threw out my perfectly good flannel shirt! So what if it had a hole in the armpit and chocolate stains on the front? It was my favorite."

THE WORKOUT

For weeks I've been preparing for an upcoming garage sale. The last one I had was five years ago, and trust me, another five years could easily pass without my repeat participation in a project that requires the exactitude of researching the technology of the microchip.

After I investigated the attic, unearthed basement boxes, and probed shelves and closet crevices, my home resembled a junkyard. Staring at the mess, I dreaded the task of organizing and pricing. But my husband offered a suggestion.

"Just price it all in groups."

"What?" I responded, ankle-deep in gaudy handbags, chipped knickknacks, and outdated clothes.

"Save yourself some work. Just separate the stuff on tables and label each table with one price and let it go at that."

Is he crazy? I wondered as I tagged and peeled tiny yellow price stickers from a sheet. Shortcuts. That's a man for you.

"Jim, you can't do that." My voice resounded with the authority and expertise of a market analyst/store manager. "Some items are more valuable than others. You can't just lump them all together."

He shrugged his shoulders as he sipped his cup of coffee. "Okay, have it your way," he said in his go-ahead-and-work-yourself-to-death tone. "But the way you're doing it is just plain silly."

When it comes to household chores, I'm a stickler for detail, and Jim is a champion of shortcuts, riddled with logic. For instance, he asks, "Why make the bed? We'll be sleeping in it again tonight."

I defend global domesticity by replying, "If you buy that theory, then why do anything? Why wash the dishes or do the laundry? Better yet, why shave, brush your teeth, or take a shower? You'll just have to do it again."

I noticed he pondered those remarks a little too

seriously. The image of awaking one morning to a disheveled mountain man scared me enough to make me stop debating the issue.

Truth is, shortcuts have their place if the end result is as good as if we went the extra mile. But when shortcuts fuel laziness and breed shoddy workmanship, they are nonproductive, even destructive, because God wants us to do our best in whatever task we perform.

That's exactly what I'm doing now, performing my best. Tagging. Sorting. Organizing. Pricing. Okay, well maybe I'm a tad obsessive with this project. I guess I could load a few tables with items of identical price.

"Jim, maybe you were. . .ah. . .right? Let's compromise. How about you help me assemble the one-dollar stuff on that table? Jim? Hello, did you hear me?"

My husband appears, this time with a canteen in hand. "You know I've been thinking. . .why have a garage sale? Why have anything? Let's give it all away, shed our repetitive routines, and live in the backwoods somewhere without all this hassle."

That's a woman for you. . .big mouth.

TARGET HEART RATE SCRIPTURE

"Whatever your hand finds to do, do it with all your might." (Or you and your resident back-woodsman could just resign yourself to live like wolves secluded from civilization.)

ECCLESIASTES 9:10

Chapter 23
RECYCLING WOES

THE WARM-UP

Words a Woman Will Never Say: "I think it's about time I carried my share of the load. I'm tired of people waiting on me."

THE WORKOUT

I dreaded the day when the waste removal service would supply us with a red recycling bin. I knew it was coming; environmental awareness was evident everywhere. It was only a matter of time before the "R" word would disrupt my dispassionate ecological attitude and force its way into my so-what-if-all-the-landfills-are-full mentality. Most neighborhoods had already been recycling for some time. How far away could it be?

Then it happened. Despite my resistance to the intrusion, our disposal service presented us with our very own red container. "Just what I need, more work. I don't have time for this!" I grumbled. "What are we supposed to do, buy another kitchen trash can just for recyclables?"

My frustrations heightened after I read the sorting instructions. "Plastic: All plastic with the recycle symbol on them including No. 1 through No. 7. Plastic Preparation: Rinse container; crush; discard cap; set in bin. Glass Preparation: Remove lids; rinse to remove residue; do not break glass; set container and lid in bin. . . ."

All right, let me get this straight. Crush plastic containers (only those numbered one through seven, mind you), and discard the caps. Do not break glass containers, but remove the lids and set both the container and the lid in the bin. Rinse all containers, not a smidgen of liquid allowed. (How about I give them a spin in the dishwasher first?) Bundle newspapers or place them in a grocery bag. But do not set them in the bin; set them beside the bin.

Curbside recycling is about as easy as reading a roadmap blindfolded. At this point I seriously considered moving to the mountains to bury our refuse. But then, I've never been good at digging ditches. What's worse, if my bin didn't show up curbside on garbage day, I'd be open game for the wrath of the environmentally righteous in the neighborhood.

But after committing to the task for a while, I noticed that recycling isn't that difficult after all. In fact, it can become as routine as sorting laundry (another favorite activity of mine).

It appears that recycling is a regular practice for the Lord, too. At times our rubbish must disgust Him. You know, the actions and attitudes that clutter our lives with sticky situations and rancid ravings? Yet He sorts and cleanses our soiled souls, disposing our self-centeredness and sin. Then He adjusts our circumstances in all the right places so that every adversity turns into something good and profitable in our lives.

Consider the tears He dries, the hearts He mends, the fragmented lives He pieces together again. Nothing is wasted in the kingdom of God, not a tear, heartache, or misfortune, not even our sinful past. God uses all things to work together for our good. When troubles litter our lives, He carefully tosses them into the recycling bin of His mercy, forgiveness, and love to create something useful and beautiful.

Hmm, perhaps recycling isn't such a bad idea after all.

TARGET HEART RATE SCRIPTURE

"And we know that in all things God works for the good of those who love him, who have been called according to his purpose." (So throw your junk into the recycling bin of God's forgiveness, and make sure you use the red bins for plastic milk containers!)   ROMANS 8:28

An Exercise in Laughter
LAUGHTER LIFTS THE SPIRIT....

Family problems were deflating our joy. "I don't know how much more I can take," I confessed to my husband as I prepared to leave the house to run errands.

"I know," he said, giving me a squeeze, "I feel the same way."

After I finished my errands, I stopped at a bookstore to search for an inspirational book. Scanning the bookshelves, I noticed a title written by an acquaintance of mine. Though not in the mood for humor, I purchased her book of lighthearted stories anyway.

At home I read the first chapter, and for the first time in weeks, I burst into laughter as the cloud of depression lifted. Still chuckling, I shared the book with my husband, and he, too, began to laugh aloud. Temporarily, we found relief as our spirits soared.

"Our mouths were filled with laughter, our tongues with songs of joy" (Psalm 126:2). I searched for inspiration, but God lifted my spirit with laughter instead.

Has depression smothered your joy? Have problems crushed your spirit? Humor is God's heart therapy. Ask yourself, *When was the last time I actually belly-laughed?*

Try this exercise:

In a small group setting, gather in
a circle and allow your brave group
leader to begin to laugh aloud while the rest of you
attempt to withhold giggles. Watch what happens!

Chapter 24
INTERMISSIONS AND VACATION DECOMPRESSION

THE WARM-UP

Words a Woman Will Never Say: "I hate the way I look with a tan. I'd much rather flaunt my pasty white skin and forgo that golden glow."

THE WORKOUT

Unlike most people, Jim and I take our vacations during the off-season. So as spring or autumn approaches, we prime our travel gear for another trip to Tucson. Tucson feels more like home than home; maybe that's why we return there so often.

Last May, for some unknown reason, I got all weepy as we drove away from our condominium to head for the Phoenix airport. My instincts were more profound than I had realized at the time. Had I known what awaited us the moment we headed for Indiana, I would have thrust myself into cataclysmic sobs instead of wimpy whimpers.

Our adventure began almost immediately. After

driving two hours to get to the Phoenix airport, we had planned to eat a late dinner before flight departure. However, the only edibles available in our terminal at 9 P.M. were dried-up hotdogs that resembled elongated prunes.

"They have a Burger King at Terminal Six," an employee suggested. So we boarded a bus to another terminal, grabbed a been-under-the-heat-lamp-too-long burger, and bused back in time to board our plane. Which just happened to be delayed two hours. At the mercy of the airline, we patiently waited for boarding time. Ten o'clock, eleven o'clock, twelve o'clock, one o'clock. Trying to muster tolerance and endurance (a giant feat for me), I kept my composure until the cacophony of screaming babies and exhausted toddlers about to board the same fully booked flight to Chicago jolted me into a panic.

"Jim, please, let's reconsider," I begged, perceiving our downhill trend. "A few more days in Arizona. That's not too much to ask, is it?" Not a chance. My husband looked at me with his common-sense-must-prevail-at-all-cost grin and our fate was sealed.

The sleepless red-eye flight to Chicago delivered us red-eyed to our wacky, wooded wonderland by late morning. Two acres of overgrown grass, fallen tree limbs, and weeds taunted us at the driveway. The refrigerator whined, "No food, fill me," the answering machine blinked more than a string of Christmas tree lights, and Mom called wanting to talk. It mattered little that we had just walked through the door, hadn't slept in twenty-four hours, and in the past eight hours had subsisted on two bags of airline peanuts, diet soda, and a burger that belonged in a doggie dish, not in one's stomach.

The rigors of home-from-vacation decompression began. Droopy-eyed and drained, I unpacked, tossed in a load of laundry, and trekked to the grocery store while Jim boarded the rider lawn mower.

Upon my return, a predictable surprise: Jim claimed the injury was minor, but a week later he underwent extensive surgery for his "ah-it's-nothing-but-a-torn-muscle-from-the-bone" mishap. As Jim recuperated, my life carried more responsibilities than a water barrel contains raindrops. Then another bolt from the blue: My dad needed surgery, too.

"I told you we shouldn't have come home." My voice held the chutzpah of a Jewish mother while Jim, in prone position, nodded a faint affirmation.

It seems the more enjoyable the time spent away, the more tempestuous the return. Yet despite the quandary, we all need a vacation or "intermission" in life. In the ongoing drama of our daily routines, intermissions are vital because they give us an opportunity to stretch our legs, buy a box of popcorn, and focus on something other than life's stage. Even God took a day of rest from His work. Although we're harried when we leave and besieged when we return, I'm grateful for the small interludes God gives us to regroup, refocus, and fortify ourselves for life's changing stage.

Ah yes, I'm ready to go. The popcorn's popping as intermission from our summer drama approaches. Who knows, maybe this time instead of just vacationing in our place of intermission, we'll exchange our wacky wooded wonderland for Tucson's center stage!

Mr. Voice of Logic just gave me another one of his common-sense-must-prevail looks again. A lot he knows. Look where his last glance got him.

Target Heart Rate Scripture

"On the seventh day he [God] rested from all his work." (I'm just hoping for a smaller dose of decompression following our next intermission.)
GENESIS 2:2

Chapter 25
JUST GEESEY

The Warm-Up

Words a Woman Will Never Say: "Gee, do you mind if I bake a few more pies for the bake sale? And I'd love to chaperone the preschoolers on their field trip if no one else would mind. It seems no one ever calls me to volunteer for anything."

The Workout

Several years ago my father-in-law made an observation as he sat at our kitchen table. "You like ducks, huh?"

"Actually, Dad, I think they're geese; but to answer your question, no, not particularly."

"Then why all the ducks. . .ah, geese?" he asked, pointing to the picture of a goose on the wall and the looming white-feathered figurine on the hutch.

"In a word," I said with a sigh, "Mom."

It began after I had made the mistake of admiring a goose figurine on my mother's piano. Little did I know my mindless comment would propel her into a buying frenzy of goose-related items for me. From then on, upon her return home from a vacation or craft exhibit, she tumbled into my hands a bounty of waterfowl treasures in various forms: geese kitchen linens and matching hand towels; plaques with cutesy poems outlined in geese; figurines of mama geese and goslings; and even a goose toothpick holder.

To breathe words remotely similar to "Gee, I like that" or "That's nice" or "Yum, that tastes good" is to issue Mom a license to buy or bake "that" until the ducks, I mean geese, fly home. Just ask my husband. Jim mistakenly told Mom that he liked her lemon cream pies. Today we could open a pastry shop with the steady supply of lemon cream pies that she bakes, chills, and carefully hand-delivers to our door.

When I could take no more, I rebelled against my webbed-feet decor and sold the geese paraphernalia in a garage sale. Then with heavy hips from ingesting lemon pie, I plopped down to devise a strategy to halt Mom's behavior. How to tactfully address the problem was a bird of another feather.

Do I issue a command? "Mom, *please,* no more geese. And by the way, Jim is fed up (pun intended) with pie." Or should I use the gentle approach and deal in half-truths: "Mom, I just love the geese stuff you've bought, but I don't think I have room for anymore."

(Forget the mention of pies on this one. Gentle confrontations allow only one truthful blow at a time.)

The command approach was too blunt; on the other hand, Mom's willful mindset has been known to skip mealy-mouthed suggestions. So I mustered up the courage and said firmly, "Please don't buy me any more geese, Mom. I have enough."

Wide-eyed, she looked up from what she was doing as if I had just committed the unpardonable sin. "I thought you liked geese."

"Yes. Ah, no. I mean. . ." I stuttered like a child hiding a bad report card. Realizing my foolishness, I spouted, "I really have enough, Mom!"

From then on I recognized my error. The Bible teaches us to mean what we say and say what we mean. Hollow words dart from my lips faster than a racehorse at the starting gate. And it costs me.

After our discussion, Mom finally quit buying me geese. However, when Mom and I shopped for a church gift exchange recently, a blouse caught my eye. "Do you like that?" she probed, staring at me with searching eyes.

I started to respond, and then I remembered. "Not really," I said with a shrug and moved to another rack.

Meanwhile, Mom picked up a purse. As she began to inspect the leather and probe the inside, I thought,

Now it's my turn. "Nice purse, huh, Ma?"

"Real nice," she replied with an inquisitive look. So when she wasn't looking, I nabbed the purse and dashed to the nearest cash register. But when I got there, I heard a familiar voice speaking to the sales-clerk. "I'd like to pay for this purse before my daughter sees it," Mom whispered.

Just ducky, I mean geesey. Move over lemon cream pie, the purse factory cometh.

TARGET HEART RATE SCRIPTURE

"Do not be quick with your mouth, do not be hasty in your heart. . .so let your words be few." (I know, I know. Enough said.)

ECCLESIASTES 5:2

Chapter 26

DO BORROWERS READ LABELS?

THE WARM-UP

Words a Woman Will Never Say: "Excuse me, Dear, but must we always talk about our feelings?"

THE WORKOUT

I use a system that seldom works. I write my name in big, bold letters on every possession that passes from my hand to another's. I do this purposely to notify the borrower that I am the owner, and, as such, I'd like the item returned. However, my message is usually ignored.

I once circulated five copies of a book I liked. Having lost books to the borrowers' sea of forgetfulness many times before, I activated a system: I inscribed my name inside the jacket cover of each book to ensure that a minimum of two or three copies would find their way back to me eventually. Today, I don't have one copy of that book, nor do I remember who borrowed them.

When my firstborn left for college, I, like any

overprotective, first-time mother of a college student, labeled his really important stuff. That way, everyone on campus was served an unwritten notice: THIS ITEM BELONGS TO THE PERSON WHOSE NAME IS ON THE LABEL, SO DON'T MESS WITH IT. Like a security guard posted at the entrance of Bloomingdale's, the labeling system was intended to repel perspective borrowers.

Sure. Like a name sewn, embossed, or printed with black indelible marker really means anything. Imagine my horror when my son returned home with a mere three-fourths of his belongings.

So I'm convinced this is the way most folks see it: If the loaned item remains in their home or office for at least sixty days, it automatically becomes the possession of the borrower. At which time, bold-printed names lose their worth in ink.

I've lost cake pans, platters, and Tupperware bowls during this sixty-day expiration period, which has forced me to stock my shelves with an assortment of who-cares-if-it-doesn't-get-returned-I-don't-want-it-anyway items such as dented aluminum pans and empty Cool Whip containers. That way, if the container never returns, it's no great loss.

I realize that lenders have better memories than borrowers, but how does one ask that an item be returned without sounding tacky? "Hey, remember the punch bowl I loaned you in 1996? I'd like it back now." Or how about the more diplomatic, albeit deceptive, approach. "By the way, do you have a punch bowl I could borrow? Seems I've misplaced mine."

There must be a system that works, but for now I simply hope for the best. In fact, just the other day I thought my system was finally beginning to take off. An acquaintance called and said, "Say, will you be home later? I have something of yours I want to return."

"Really?" I said with gleeful anticipation. "What is it?"

"Two giant Cool Whip containers," she replied.

Seems I got carried away with my permanent marker. But that's okay. I told her to wait sixty days.

TARGET HEART RATE SCRIPTURE

" 'Give to those who ask, and don't turn away from those who want to borrow.' " (But definitely keep an ample supply of markers on hand.)

MATTHEW 5:42 TLB

Chapter 27
WOMEN IN THE MEN'S ROOM

THE WARM-UP

Words a Woman Will Never Say: "Do you believe she had the gall to buy me a basket of assorted scented soaps, bath beads, and dusting powder for my personal shower? Does she think that I plan to bathe on my honeymoon?"

THE WORKOUT

My daughters-in-law and I had attended a Christian conference for women held at the United Center in Chicago. Since the event hosted thousands of women in need of ample restroom facilities, the coordinators opened the men's restrooms to accommodate the ladies. Aside from the time when I mistakenly entered the men's room at the airport, this was my first bona fide visit to the interior of such a place.

Now when women get bored, any topic of discussion is not only reasonable but inevitable. After waiting in a very long line for a very long time, restlessness hit the restroom with gale force. I'm ashamed to say that the boredom brainstorming began with me. As I edged closer to the meager two stalls, I faced a line of urinals across the opposite wall. To my disgrace, I tried to figure out the purpose for the four-by-four-inch shelf I noticed above several of the porcelain potties.

Silent curiosity provoked me to speak as I nonchalantly turned to the stranger behind me, who also faced the wall of white porcelain. "What do you think those square shelves are for?" I asked in a moment of mindless spontaneity. To my amazement and relief, she had been pondering the same question.

"I think they're ashtrays," she replied.

"Oh no," a lady three women behind us chided. "See? There's a 'No Smoking' sign, so it couldn't be an ashtray."

I resisted the urge to instruct the law-abiding lady that most men don't see, let alone obey those types of signs, while another woman offered her assessment. "It's for their wallets," she said flatly.

"Could be," I countered, "but don't men usually keep their wallets in their back pockets?"

The entire line of women now faced the line of urinals as the debate escalated and one woman after another gave her not-so-expert opinion on the use of the tiny platform.

A stall finally opened and I took my turn as the ladies continued to discuss the unsolved mystery. En route to wash my hands, I walked past the shelf and gave it another glance. "A cup holder," another woman offered. Doubtful, I volleyed another negative. "Wouldn't the shelf be circular to fit the cup's base?" I said as I lathered and rinsed.

As I exited the restroom, the discussion that I initiated from a case of the doldrums continued among the women still waiting in line. And who could predict how or when it would end?

Women differ from men drastically, and not in just the obvious ways. Men would dismiss our discussion as foolish babble, but not women. We are problem-solvers and solution-finders. We like answers, and we seek closure.

Spiritually, those characteristics serve us well. When a family need arises and life's storms brew, we persist in prayer long after most men fold up their tents and move on. We linger long at the bedside of a sick child or elderly parent, and we don't give up easily.

So in true form, I persisted. I brought the unsolved mystery question home to the man I deem an authority in these matters. "Honey," I said, having just returned from the conference, "what are those square stainless steel shelves above the urinals for?"

My husband glanced at me with raised eyebrows. "I thought you went to a women's conference. . . . What were you doing in the men's room?"

After I explained and my husband breathed a giant sigh of relief, I repeated the question. "I have no idea," he said with a blank stare. It was apparent that he didn't care, either.

Typical. I'll bet he's never noticed the "No Smoking" sign, either.

TARGET HEART RATE SCRIPTURE

" 'I will explain to you the mystery of the woman.' " (Are we that complex? The shelf question. . .now that's the real mystery.)

REVELATION 17:7

Chapter 28
SUPPORT BLOCKS

THE WARM-UP

Words a Woman Will Never Say: "I'm delighted when something in my home breaks down. It allows me the joyful experience of going without necessities for long periods of time while I wait for the repairman to show up."

THE WORKOUT

My paranoia emerges over the dumbest things. The other day I glanced up from our bed and noticed the ceiling fan whirling and wobbling. Immediately my thoughts confirmed the obvious. Whirling is good. Wobbling is bad.

I made the initial observation when the electrician first installed it. "The other ceiling fans you installed don't wobble," I noted, as the no-nonsense handyman descended the ladder. Swiftly he handed me the plastic bag that contained the warranty and other information I never read.

"There's weights in there."

"Weights?"

"Yep," he said, folding the ladder and moving toward the door. "They balance the blades to stop the wobble."

"Where do I place the weights?" I probed, hinting for some professional assistance. A devilish grin accompanied his fragmented reply. "Better work with it. Not easy to do."

Interpretation: Not easy to do as in, "Go ahead, lady. Position those tiny metal weights in every imaginable angle and watch that fan wobble. Move them fastidiously to another angle, and another, and still another. Tear your hair out. Sweat bullets. Spend hours decoding the instructions. Hire mathematical geniuses to formulate hypotheses to stop the wobble. It will still (he-he-he) wobble."

Enter paranoia: my husband and I lying asleep in the security of our bedroom as the ceiling fan whirls and wobbles above us. Then in the dead of night, the five-blade brass and glass fan and light fixture crashes upon our unconscious bodies, severing limbs and crippling us for life, thus giving birth to deep-rooted fanophobic tendencies thereafter.

As I was absorbed in grizzly mental pictures, my silence astonished the electrician to actually speak a full sentence. "It'll be okay the way it is." His flash of humanitarianism startled me.

"You mean there's no danger of the fan falling down?"

His impish grin dissolved into an I-don't-believe-this-nut-case smirk. "Nah, it's up there good, fastened onto a support block."

The support block theory temporarily calmed my insanity. Funny thing about human beings. We need support. Just enough reassurance to make us feel as if everything—despite the appearance—will be fine.

Sure the surgery is serious, but it's a common procedure today. Doctors perform it as often as they set broken bones. More important, friends and family are praying for you. A support block.

Yes, the kids need new school clothes, the car just broke down, and you just got transferred again. But that nest egg you saved helps, and so will the church with a special loving offering. Thoughtful and loving support blocks.

Yes, you've made some bad choices. You feel as if you have failed God, your family, and yourself. But remember, Jesus loves, forgives, and understands you. A soul-saving support block.

"It's up there good, fastened to a support block." The electrician's words continue to offer me comfort. With

our faith fastened to God, we, too, are fastened securely to His eternal stability. Rest assured, despite our fluctuations and wavering ways, God bolsters us with His constant care. Like my ceiling fan, we might wobble occasionally, but we won't fall down.

TARGET HEART RATE SCRIPTURE

"We are hard pressed on every side, but not crushed; perplexed, but not in despair; persecuted, but not abandoned; struck down, but not destroyed." (Whirling and wobbling, but not falling down.)　　2 CORINTHIANS 4:8–9

Chapter 29

WHEN LIFE VOIDS YOUR COUPONS

The Warm-Up

Words a Woman Will Never Say: "Grocery shopping, what a rush! What I like most is waiting in long lines for price checks and pushing a cart with a cockeyed wheel. One tests my patience and the other strengthens my biceps."

The Workout

Saving coupons: It works for some but not for me. However, there was a time in my life when I actually clipped the little pieces of paper and used them. I even toted a coupon carrier, complete with Velcro closure and scissors compartment.

On each trip to the grocery store, I packed my purple pouch, eager to redeem stacks of perfectly clipped coupons. Enthusiastically, I entered the grocery store, braced for a two-hour excursion. As I weaved in and out of every aisle, I flipped through my bulging file of categorically arranged coupons while eyeing brands of canned veggies, fruit drinks, and toilet bowl cleaners. Shopping turned into a game of concentration as I wracked my brain to recall if I possessed a coupon to match the prospective product. Other shoppers whisked by, grinning wryly as I sorted through a fistful of cat food coupons, comparing cans with the corresponding stubs. "Save $1.00," one coupon read, "when you buy thirty or more cans of. . ." But I remained undaunted. The time I spent was well worth it. After all, we're talking big savings here. Or so I thought.

Finally after hours of flipping, scanning, and comparing, I headed for the checkout counter. Replete with self-satisfaction, I collected my coupons to present to the cashier. Only, I often forgot to check one small detail the conscientious cashier seldom forgot.

With an eerie tone of vindictive delight, speaking loud enough for everyone to hear, she'd announce, "Sorry, Ma'am, I can't accept these coupons. They've expired."

Assuring her I didn't mean to cheat her, the store, the manufacturer, or the world in general, I stuffed the worthless coupons in my purse, paid full price for the items, and left. Defeated. In an instant, several hours of frugality were whisked away faster than the time it takes my family to scarf down a meal that took me all day to prepare. So much for savings.

Life sometimes treats us the same way. We strive to plan, organize, and save, but often our work is in vain. We spend years working to build our savings, our job security, and our homes, only to lose everything when a slight shift in the winds of circumstance whisks it all away.

"Sorry," the boss says. "Your position has expired."

"Wish I could help you," the banker sighs, "but. . ."

Discouraged, we reevaluate our lives, groping for understanding and wondering if everything we have worked so hard to accomplish has been a waste of time.

Although life is full of uncertainties, God offers encouragement and hope to those who invest their lives in Him. Even when life's cashier rejects our coupons, tossing our hard work to the wind, God assures us our investment in His work is never lost.

And we're talking big savings here.

TARGET HEART RATE SCRIPTURE

"Therefore, my dear brothers, stand firm. Let nothing move you. Always give yourselves fully to the work of the Lord, because you know that your labor in the Lord is not in vain." (Which is more than I can say about clipping and sorting coupons.)   1 CORINTHIANS 15:58

Chapter 30
FRAGILE CARGO TRAVELING HOME

THE WARM-UP

Words a Woman Will Never Say: "I plan to decorate my home in a hospital corridor motif: cold, congested, and uninviting."

THE WORKOUT

There's nothing more nerve-racking than driving a loved one home from the hospital after he or she has undergone major surgery. Fears stumble through your head as you, ever so cautiously, careen away from the hospital entrance with fragile cargo aboard. One tiny fender bender could cause unthinkable consequences to the patient in your care.

Following my husband's spinal surgery, the doctor instructed Jim not to drive or ride in a car for weeks. "Any jarring to the spinal cord could cause permanent paralysis," the doctor warned.

Thank you, Doctor, for this final instruction on the verge of transporting my husband fifty-plus miles through

Chicago Loop traffic, rush-hour traffic, local traffic, and then (whew) home.

I can do this, I told myself. *No I can't!* myself snapped back. So my dad, like a kamikaze pilot volunteering for a death mission, sacrificially offered to take the wheel.

Sitting erect, Jim was strapped to the front seat like a prisoner propped in an electric chair awaiting execution. The bulky neck brace forced his head straight and center. I sat in the backseat directly behind him, slamming my foot on an imaginary brake whenever Dad edged too close to other vehicles.

Meanwhile, I held my breath and vocalized injunctions to drivers who invaded our road space. "Hey there, Fella, stay in your own lane! Watch it, wa–a–atch it! Put your turn signal on, Lady! Quit huggin' our bumper, Mister!"

By the time we arrived home, I was hyperventilating and felt as if I needed an oxygen mask and professional help. As a result, I invented an idea that should be patented—a huge protective bubble covering the car with a sign, required by law, posted on the outside, warning, "SLOW MOVING VEHICLE. HOSPITAL PATIENT TRAVELING HOME. AN AUTOMATIC EXPULSION OF NAILS AND OTHER SHARP OBJECTS WILL DAMAGE ANY CAR THAT COMES WITHIN TEN

FEET OF THIS VEHICLE'S ROAD SPACE."

Anything to avoid the unthinkable.

In the same way, imagine if we would consider the consequences of exercising poor judgment, unwise decisions, or thoughtless words before haphazardly stumbling into senseless behavior. What if we guarded our spirit at any cost? I wonder what positive results we'd glean?

The Bible teaches that if we'll obey God's Word, blessings will follow. We carry the precious cargo of a soul and spirit in these timeworn bodies of ours. After the body dies, our spirit travels on, its destination determined by our acceptance or rejection of the gospel of Christ. So it pays to take preventive measures to guard our souls and heed the instructions of the Great Physician. Our life's journey to our final destination is a lot less complicated and a lot more enjoyable that way.

Hmm. How about creating a device to avoid spiritual disaster from encroaching on us? An unseen warning sign written on our hearts declaring: *Slow to anger, slow to speak, Christian traveling home. Evil thoughts or actions that come within ten feet will be instantly demolished.*

Might work. Anything to avoid the unthinkable.

LAUGHTER THERAPY

TARGET HEART RATE SCRIPTURE

"Be swift to hear, slow to speak, slow to wrath."
(And eager to follow God's warning signs.)

JAMES 1:19 KJV

Chapter 31
HOMEBUILDERS ANONYMOUS

THE WARM-UP

Words a Woman Will Never Say: "My husband is too good at replacing the empty ketchup bottles I leave in the refrigerator or the empty toilet tissue roll I don't have time to change. I'd like to contribute something to our household. But he's so efficient and conscientious, I have nothing to do all day but enjoy my surroundings."

THE WORKOUT

He called to confirm the order on the kitchen cabinets for our new home. He was one of the few real competent salesmen with whom I had the rare pleasure to do business.

"How are you?" he asked.

"Fine," I said, lying. "Well, not really. I'm a mess."

"Getting to ya, huh?" he replied, as one who dealt with homebuilders on a regular basis. He then told me that he had just spoken with several other homebuilders who confided that if they had known what building a home entailed, they would have never started in the first place.

"Who are they? I want to talk to them!" I countered.

So I'm starting a support group never devised before: Homebuilders Anonymous. I can see it now. Weary and worn from the rigors of nonstop construction frustrations, I step to a podium in front of a crowd of other droopy-eyed, disheveled, former "together" people and stutter, "I–I'm Tina. And I–I'm a homebuilder."

The group applauds. Some nod their heads in affirmation. Others grab handkerchiefs from their purses or pockets to wipe their moistened eyes. Meanwhile, other more unfortunate souls sit in a trancelike state, twitching uncontrollably.

Custom homebuilding produces nagging frustrations such as contractors' broken promises (lots of them), adverse weather conditions (lots of it), incompetent salespeople (an overabundance of them), wrong deliveries (had some), wrong orders made by incompetent salespeople (had more than some), and delays, delays, delays due to all of the above.

So after I had just swept three inches of water from our plywood floors for the fourth time in several days, nailed plastic to the window openings where windows should have been weeks ago, and finished arguing with the vinyl siding salesman for selling our reserved and prepaid siding to someone else, I was comforted to know that other homebuilders shared similar frustrations.

The old adage claims that misery loves company. But I'd like to think of it another way. The Scriptures say our trials equip us to help others who face the same adversities as we do. Just as God comforts us, we are called to comfort others.

Having observed our mounting construction frustrations, our good-hearted carpenter Adam and his wife Kelly gave us a call. "You need a night out," Kelly stated. "How about if we treat you to dinner?"

Droopy-eyed and drained, my husband and I gratefully accepted. You see, Adam and Kelly understand homebuilding. A few years ago they built a new home and survived.

We had a great evening. My husband and I unloaded as Adam and Kelly nodded their heads in affirmation and pulled out their handkerchiefs to dab their moistened eyes. More important, their encouragement and support assured us that after the process ends, our experience will enable us to comfort future homebuilders like ourselves.

But maybe I ought to curb this uncontrollable twitching first.

LAUGHTER THERAPY

TARGET HEART RATE SCRIPTURE

"Praise be to the God and Father of our Lord Jesus Christ. . .who comforts us in all our troubles, so that we can comfort those. . .with the comfort we ourselves have received from God." (And from former homebuilders like Kelly and Adam.)

2 CORINTHIANS 1:3–4

Chapter 32
TROUBLE IN PARADISE

THE WARM-UP

Words a Woman Will Never Say: "Must we always vacation in Hawaii? Can't we visit somewhere more exciting and adventurous. . .like, say, the Bermuda Triangle?"

THE WORKOUT

"Aloha, welcome to paradise," the flight attendant announced as our plane touched down on the exotic island of Maui, Hawaii.

All my life I heard people sing the praises of beautiful, enchanting Hawaii. Some went so far as to say that it reflected the beauty of heaven itself. Now it was my turn to experience its celestial enchantment as my family and I embarked upon our first tropical adventure.

Driving to our condominium, we absorbed every morsel of scenery. The scenes were just as I imagined— a dazzling blue sky with barely a cloud to interrupt the flow of deep, rich color. Flowering shrubs dotted the wayside. Tall palm trees swayed in the brisk trade winds, and sun-kissed beaches lined the highway to our left while rugged mountain terrains painted a panoramic view to our right. Paradise!

Soon, however, our celestial visions shattered as Hawaii's earthly elements emerged. Shortly after our arrival, we sighted a roach in our posh, oceanfront condo.

All right, but everything else was *so* beautiful. Surely I could dismiss one insect and enjoy—"What did you say is crawling inside the living room?" I yelled to my husband from another room when I heard him mutter something. "A lizard?"

"No, no," he said. "I said one of those little geckos seems to have made its way into our living room."

Watching the critter scamper across the ceiling, I shouted, "I don't care about its proper name, it's a lizard!"

After eliminating all visible critters, I doused the floorboards and entryways with a can of extra-strength Raid. Attempting to maintain a positive attitude, I resolved to avert any future problems by refrigerating everything. That included boxed cereals, dishes, flatware, and any other item that would go from hand to mouth, just in case the unwanted critters had family in the area (and they always do). But I maintained a positive attitude. After all, this was "paradise."

Days later I discovered another island attraction. Gazing upward, I noticed aluminum sheeting wrapped around the palm trees. "What's that for?" I asked my brother, a longtime resident of Maui.

"Oh," he said casually, "that's to prevent rats from climbing the trees."

"Rats?"

"Uh-huh, they're a problem in tropical climates."

By now, only three words expressed my feelings: trouble in paradise.

Interesting how we clamor for a piece of heaven on earth when in reality even the most beautiful surroundings are flawed. Consequently, our search for perfection in an imperfect world often leads to discouragement.

Yet God promises us a place of beauty unequaled by anything we have ever experienced on earth. A place where sin, sickness, sorrow (as well as rats, roaches, and geckos) cease to exist, a true paradise called heaven.

Whenever this earthly life troubles me, I hold on to that assurance. Meanwhile, a can of Raid is never far from my grasp.

Target Heart Rate Scripture

Jesus said, " 'In my Father's house are many mansions: if it were not so, I would have told you. I go to prepare a place for you.' " (Where there is no trouble in paradise.)   JOHN 14:2 KJV

An Exercise in Laughter

LAUGHTER BREAKS THE TENSION. . . .

On his trip to Japan, President Ronald Reagan received pressure from the Japanese government to implement more favorable trade concessions. Frustrated, the Japanese officials tried to change the president's mind by using guilt. "We never bombed one of your U.S. cities," they reminded him.

With that, the quick-witted Reagan replied, "Oh yeah? What about Detroit?" The entire assembly broke into laughter, defusing the tension.

Try this exercise:

In a group, share how humor defused a tense situation in your life.

Then brainstorm: What are some tension-breakers you can use this week? Sharing a funny quip with a coworker? Baking happy-face cookies for your spouse after a disagreement?

Humor breaks tension while restoring our perspective at the same time!

Chapter 33
GET MOVING

THE WARM-UP

Words a Woman Will Never Say: "The insects that invade my kitchen are fascinating. Their tiny legs and delicate translucent wings are so cute!"

THE WORKOUT

"What's wrong with us?" I asked my husband after another frustrating start to a few days away. It seems wherever we go, the first day is a disaster and we end up moving.

Our quirky ways are particularly frustrating to my husband, because once he sits down somewhere, anywhere, he's home. Not me. If a theater seat is too close to the front, too far in the back, or not centered enough in the middle, I move. If our restaurant table is too close to the smoking section, too cramped, or too near the general traffic pattern, we find another.

So after much research, we rented a quaint mountain cabin. After the long drive up a steep, winding

road, we arrived. I toured each room while my husband deposited our luggage in the master bedroom upstairs.

Instantly I noticed a few things I didn't like, but, hey, we were in the mountains and I could ignore a few dead ladybugs, couldn't I? And sure the cabin wasn't as clean as I would have liked it, but I do tend to nitpick too much. I tried to hide my misgivings, but my discomfort showed more than a black slip under a white dress.

Soon, Jim's oh-no-she-doesn't-like-the-place antenna detected my dissatisfaction, and, as if on cue, he bounced into his overly positive mode. "Wow, will you look at this great view?" he said with a sunbeam smile, attempting to derail my negativity. "There's nothing like this at home!"

"Uh-huh," I muttered motionless, examining the room with x-ray eyes.

Another attempt: "How about I start a fire?" He continued to beam as he opened the flue, crumpled newspaper, and searched for matches. Trying my best to adjust, I pretended all was well, despite the crumbs on the couch cushions, the sticky glass ring on the coffee table, and a gap in the front door frame wide enough to accommodate several sizable rodents.

Jim struggled to start a fire, blowing the blackened newspaper with mighty huffs and puffs, as I trudged upstairs to unpack. Placing the suitcase on the bed, I noticed the sheets had not been changed from the previous guests. Disgusted, as I stripped off the old linens and changed the bedding, I noticed several wasps buzzing in the bay window.

After finding a can of insecticide, I sprayed and swatted as I hung up our clothes in the cedar-lined closet. Afterward, I entered the bathroom, where, in the mirror's reflection, I saw a steady stream of insects storming out of the closet where I had just hung our clothes.

"Jim!" I screamed from the upstairs balcony; he was still bent over hearthside. "Come quick! There's a hoard of wasps in here!"

Instantly, a rain cloud darkened Jim's sunny disposition. Nearly hyperventilating from trying to start a fire with green wood and few matches, Jim surrendered to the more challenging task of a hysterical wife and a swarm of stinging insects.

The next morning we packed up to relocate. "What's wrong with us?" Jim echoed my question as he hoisted our luggage into the SUV. "Sounds like a case of Proverbs 21:9 to me."

"I hate it when you get sarcastically theological," I countered, sensing the Scripture verse was less than flattering. "Let's move before another rain cloud comes."

LAUGHTER THERAPY

TARGET HEART RATE SCRIPTURE

"Better to live on a corner of the roof than share a house with a quarrelsome wife." (Or worse yet, to share a cabin with a swarm of flying insects!)

PROVERBS 21:9

Chapter 34
A THORN OF A CARPET CLEANER

THE WARM-UP

Words a Woman Will Never Say: "What I enjoy most about a quiet evening alone is the time and opportunity I have to answer phone solicitors' questions and pledge donations to any organization who knocks at my door."

THE WORKOUT

He came to shampoo my carpets. "Just the living room, dining room, hallway, and stairs," I instructed the carpet cleaner as I withdrew to my office.

"Got a special going today," he urged, dismissing my directions. "We'll clean two chairs for the price of one."

"No thanks, just the two rooms, hallway, and stairs," I repeated.

An hour later, the whir of the shampooer stopped, and a head peered around the doorway to my office. "Say. . .any bedroom carpets need cleaning?"

"No thank you," I said, absorbed in my work.

"I'll clean a bedroom carpet for the price of the hallway," he prodded.

The man was becoming a nuisance and I was losing my patience. "All right," I said with a sigh, "but that's it."

When he finally finished the job, he asked if he could use the telephone. Eager to finalize things and get back to work, I endorsed the check as he made his call. Overhearing his conversation, I became skeptical; and after he hung up, I asked if the call was local.

"Ah–h–h," he stuttered, "it was to our Blue Island office."

"That's long distance!" I snapped. "I hope you plan to pay for the call."

Innocent and wide-eyed, he gave me the conventional line. "Company policy prohibits me from doing that, Ma'am. You'll have to contact the customer service department."

"What's the number?" I snapped, getting more upset by the minute.

"It's on the invoice," he answered, as he handed me the receipt that showed he overcharged me for his services.

"I thought you said the bedroom would be the same price as the hallway? You charged me for an additional room!" I barked.

With my adrenaline flowing like molten lava, I just about tossed him out on his Clean 'n' Vac. His pushiness and unprofessionalism released my most venomous emotions. Frankly, I was ashamed of myself after he left.

In the Book of Corinthians, the Apostle Paul spoke of a thorn in his flesh—a physical condition God had allowed to keep Paul dependent upon Him. Obviously, the condition was an uncomfortable annoyance to Paul; it reminded him of his own vulnerabilities and imperfections. Though Paul prayed for the thorn's removal, God refused, assuring Paul that God's grace was sufficient.

The uncomfortable prick of a "thorn in the flesh" comes in different forms. The thorn of illness, financial strain, or family problems often punctures our sense of well-being, plummeting us into unrest. That's when our true character rises to the surface.

Unfortunately for me, when the "thorn" of an incompetent carpet cleaner spurred me the wrong way, impatience and anger surfaced like a pair of shark fins slicing through water. But like Paul, I realize that God exposes my weaknesses so that He can turn them into strengths.

So I guess thorns are necessary. I just wish the next one would pay for his long-distance phone call.

LAUGHTER THERAPY

TARGET HEART RATE SCRIPTURE

" 'My grace is sufficient for you, for my power is made perfect in weakness.' " *(But must you use such aggravating thorns, Lord?)*

2 CORINTHIANS 12:9

Chapter 35
BAKING COOKIES? BAH! HUMBUG!

THE WARM-UP

What a Woman Will Never Say: "Raindrops on washed windows and whiskers in the sink; timers and doorbells driving me to the brink; bright paper packages damaged with knicks and dings, these are a few of my favorite things."

THE WORKOUT

"This year, no cookie baking!" my eighty-year-old mom chided as we discussed holiday plans. I agreed.

Last year my daughter-in-law Robin decided to host a Christmas cookie-baking day. "Wouldn't it be fun for all the women in our family to get together to bake cookies?" she asked eagerly.

For Robin, Christmas conjures old-fashioned Norman Rockwell scenes of crackling fires, steamy mugs of hot chocolate, and the scent of homemade cookies and holiday breads wafting through the house. Gathered around an old upright piano, family members lift their steamy mugs and mismatched voices in song. Void of chaos, dirty dishes, and crumpled wrapping paper, the cozy scenes are stress-free and serene.

My Christmas images differ slightly. Having hosted more events than Martha Stewart and juggled enough pots and pans to make Julia Child look like a kitchen klutz, I looked forward to an entire day of mixing, baking, and decorating about as much as I welcomed a fly in my cookie mix. But in an attempt not to squelch Robin's youthful enthusiasm and holiday spirit, Mom and I agreed.

As the day approached, Robin's excitement escalated. Preparing for the event, she made lists of things we would need to bring. "Oh, by the way," she added, "I don't have a rolling pin. Could you bring yours? And would you mind bringing some extra mixing bowls and measuring spoons? And do you already have sprinkles? If not, I'll buy some more. . . ." Each day she added more items to her list as the phone rang with her requests.

Finally the day arrived. When I picked up Mom, it took all of half an hour to load her bags of bakery gadgets into my car. Seems Mom received a few phone calls, too. Shifting boxes and bags to make room, I squeezed Mom's stuff in with mine.

When we arrived at Robin's, she greeted us at the

door with smiles and holiday cheer. "Can I help you bring things in?" she asked warmly as Mom and I trudged to and from the car, handing her bag after bag. Soon my other daughter-in-law, Theresa, arrived, hauling in her carload of bakery items, too. Much like our hostess, Theresa couldn't wait to begin our bake-'til-you-break extravaganza.

Only one problem: Mom and I were already ready to break. But like busy holiday elves, we emptied bags, sorted, and set up our workstations while the festive strains of "Joy to the World" played in the background.

After hours of rolling, sifting, sprinkling, and stirring, the "older" ladies slowed down and ambled to the living room for some Christmas carols minus the mayhem. Meanwhile the youthful duo laughed and whirled around the kitchen like two pixies on a sugar surge.

"I'm exhausted," I said as I eased into a chair.

"I am, too," Mom replied, resting her head against the back of the couch. "You know, I just can't keep up like I used to."

Suddenly, the girls noticed our disappearance. "Hey, where'd you guys go?" Robin yelled through the house.

"Yeah," Theresa echoed. "Why'd you stop baking?"

I shifted into my philosophical mode. Why'd we stop baking? Might it have anything to do with the fact that for thirty-plus years on my part and more than a half century for Mom, we have baked and cooked until our wooden spoons squared off at the end and our white rubber spatulas turned yellow? Could it be that Christmas carols and warm fuzzy scenes lose their glow in a cloud of white flour and confectioner's sugar?

"Bah! Humbug! to the baking scene," I mumbled under my breath. But I kept my voice low, like a subdued Scrooge. "We're coming," I assured the girls with a sigh as Mom and I lifted our sagging bodies with simultaneous groans.

At the end of the day, I determined to simplify the holiday process in the future and concentrate on the real meaning of the season—the coming of Jesus Christ to this earth to redeem us from our sins.

However, I am relieved the younger set has the energy and enthusiasm for the blessed holiday season. And I must admit, a symphony of Christmas carols intermingled with the aroma of hot-out-of-the-oven cookies is warm and inviting—as long as I am eating, not baking them. By the way, Mom just seconded that.

LAUGHTER THERAPY

TARGET HEART RATE SCRIPTURE

" 'Do not be afraid. I bring you good news of great joy that will be for all the people. Today in the town of David a Savior has been born to you; he is Christ the Lord.' " (And unlike a day of cookie baking, that's cause for enthusiasm and excitement!)   LUKE 2:10–11

Chapter 36
NO MAKEUP DAY

THE WARM-UP

Words a Woman Will Never Say: "I prefer to reveal my age spots and facial flaws so that my true inner beauty is free to shine through."

THE WORKOUT

"Oh, it was glorious," my friend beamed as she told me about her no makeup day. I was envious. The thought of awaking in the morning to snub my cosmetic case was more enticing to me than feasting on a box of chocolates in the midst of a sugar attack.

But before I could schedule "my day," I had to mentally prepare myself. *Men don't worry about cosmetics, so why should women?* I reasoned. *Besides, why gob mascara on perfectly clean eyelashes and draw dark lines on my eyelids like a road map? Yeah, that's right! I'm tired of painting my face to please others! El natural is the real me!*

All pumped up, my day arrived. Eager to nix my

feminine fixation, I tossed my powder puff and blush brush to the wind. Gleefully, I splashed water on my face, patted it dry, swept my hair into a tousled pony-tail, and voila! Freedom. Barefaced and beautiful (all in the eye of the beholder, remember?), I faced my face with confidence.

But soon my protest posed a slight problem. It began with the doorbell. On my day of nonconformity a pushy salesman and two unexpected visitors flocked to my door to test my resolve. Feeling less confident, I scurried to the grocery store for a gallon of milk, hop-ing I wouldn't see anyone I knew. Not a chance. There she was in all her flawless beauty and fashion flare, an acquaintance I hadn't seen in years. As I lurked behind a store display, she flagged me down, gushing with waves and chatter.

"Well hello! How are you?" she surged with her cover-girl smile, as I struggled to adjust my lopsided ponytail. In true freedom, I apologized for my appear-ance, assuring her I never look that way. But I doubt she heard me.

Driving home, I began to question my glorious makeupless state, but I gave myself a short pep talk. With new resolve, I attacked the rest of my day with renewed assurance. After all, I was safely home now.

Peering out the front window, I noticed the mail

truck pull away, so I walked outside to the mailbox. Right on cue, my neighbor pulled out of his driveway to leave his house. I knew I could get by with a brief wave, but just in case, I bowed my head to sort through my stack of mail as if I hadn't noticed him. No go. This was the one time he stopped to talk, which meant I had to approach his car, giving him an up-close-and-personal view of my barefaced state. Not only that, I had just eaten a kosher dill with lunch, which meant my breath reeked of pickle juice. Preoccupied with my sloppy appearance and pungent pickle breath, I had no idea what he said.

No more pep talks. The moment I stepped indoors, I dashed to the bathroom to brush my teeth, style my hair, and apply the Maybelline, even though I knew I wouldn't see another soul all day. It mattered little. The act of primping compensated for how humiliated I felt after allowing the masses to see me pale-faced and frumpy.

Funny thing about nonconformity; unless you believe in your cause, the act is more ineffective than the roar of a toothless lion. Similar to our walk with the Lord. We believe in Jesus Christ, yet do we demonstrate our faith through corresponding deeds? When we defy conformity to the world, we should be unashamed to speak the truth even when challenged, faced with opposition, or when things occur to test our resolve. Our convictions come from the heart, based on the truth of God's Word, so negativity fails to intimidate us. Unlike my makeupless state, our spiritual transparency doesn't humiliate us; rather, we freely communicate the gospel despite our flaws.

Good point to remember the next time I risk another no makeup day. Insecurity, humiliation, and lack of conviction quell the whole meaning behind cosmetic abstinence. Add to that the scent of pickle juice, and nonconformity takes on a whole, ah, new complexion. . . .

TARGET HEART RATE SCRIPTURE

"Faith without works is dead." (And a day without makeup is anything but glorious!)

JAMES 2:20 KJV

Chapter 37
A PILLOW PLEASER

THE WARM-UP

Words a Woman Will Never Say: "It delighted me to find a mouse beneath my kitchen sink. The furry critter is the perfect, inexpensive pet for my nephew."

THE WORKOUT

"This is not my pillow," my husband huffed as he climbed into bed.

"Yes it is, Dear," I replied calmly. "I washed it today."

He examined it closer. "It can't be," he insisted. "It's full of lumps and bumps. My pillow doesn't have lumps."

I explained that the lumps were from washing it and assured him that, in time, the lumps would flatten out. Unconvinced, he pounded his fist into the bulges. "How can I sleep on this thing? It doesn't even fold in half."

This scene was a replay of several nights before. Déjà vu all over again.

My husband's dingy, dirty pillow was beginning

to become a health threat. Since the pillow is one of those never-throw-away items my husband clings to like a security blanket, I tried to dispose of it with the use of some well-intentioned trickery. Foolhardily, I rummaged through the closet for a suitable pillow replacement. Anything was better than the smelly one he had. Finally, I found a pillow that met all of the requirements: used, but in decent, broken-in condition, bending-in-half flexibilities intact, and flat but soft. Perfect. He'd never know the difference, I thought.

Happily, I skipped outdoors to dispose of the old pillow. I wrapped it in a trash bag and buried it deep within the garbage container.

That night I held my breath and waited for a response as my husband climbed into bed. As usual, he bent his pillow in half and positioned his head squarely in the middle.

Silence. I'd thought I'd pulled it off until he groaned, "This is *not* my pillow." At that point I had a choice to make—I could lie or fess up. Reluctantly, I chose the latter but not without a fight. "Honey, please. . .just give it a chance. Your other pillow has seen its day," I argued.

We debated for several minutes before I surrendered. Early the next morning, I trudged outside to retrieve the original. I washed it several times, but after enduring the dryer cycle, it came out looking like a giant wadded ball.

Tired of trying to please, I made a halfhearted attempt to smooth the lumps as I slipped a pillowcase over the clean but bumpy pillow. I tossed the ball on the bed and braced myself for round two of another spousal uprising at nightfall.

I think it was St. Augustine who said, "Habits, if not resisted, soon become a necessity." My husband's habitual nightly ritual of pillow positioning has become his necessity and my nemesis. But women are accustomed to that. For a while, we try to accommodate our husband, our children, our parents, our friends, our pastor, and everyone in between, in futile attempts to please. Tired and drained, wisdom finally prevails as we put to rest our concerns and leave the lumps and bumps to settle on their own.

As my husband pounds his fist into the pillow and squeezes it to fold it in half, I curl up on my side and breathe deeply. "I don't know why you had to wash it," he moans. "How will I ever be able to sleep on this?"

With a yawn, I close my eyes. "Good night, Dear," I say warmly.

"Good night," he responds flatly.

A few minutes pass before gentle snores rise from

the lumps and bumps. Wisdom prevails as the pillow issue smooths out on its own.

TARGET HEART RATE SCRIPTURE

"Am I now trying to win the approval of men, or of God? Or am I trying to please men?" (Unfortunately, I'm trying to do a little of both.)

GALATIANS 1:10

Three

FUNNY WEIGHT-WATCHING MOMENTS

Chapter 38

WE'RE TRIM, WE'RE FIT, WE'RE DROWNING!

THE WARM-UP

Words a Woman Will Never Say: "I'm so envious. Carol gained another twenty pounds and all I do is lose, lose, lose. Before you know it, I'll be wearing a size 8! Then I'll have to buy a whole new wardrobe. How depressing."

THE WORKOUT

"We won't take long," my husband assured the lifeguard, convincing her to allow us to swim a few laps before the pool opened. Reluctantly, she agreed but informed us that pool rules required her to watch us. No problem. Or so we thought.

It was our first full vacation day at the Broadmoor Hotel in Colorado Springs. Jogging fanatics that we were at the time, we rejoiced when we checked in and noticed a walking path that encircled a lake and an Olympic-size pool. In those days exercise was a high priority, even on vacations. We routinely jogged a few miles and swam laps before starting the day.

This vacation was no different with one exception: None of the motel pools we had experienced before compared to this one. Awaking to the brisk Rocky Mountain air, we jogged an exhilarating three miles. Then, after the lifeguard gave us the okay, we dashed upstairs to change into our swimsuits. *Yep, we're trim, we're fit, and we're ready to swim those laps,* I gloated.

The lifeguard climbed atop her elevated chair while we stretched, making broad circles with our straightened arms. The length of the pool sprawled before us like a sea of glass sparkling in the morning sun. Goggles affixed and in true athletic form, we began our Olympic laps. Or should I say lap. . .or perhaps a more accurate description would be half-lap. Actually, midpool I was treading water, trying to appear collected.

I glanced ahead and saw Jim having trouble, too. Humiliated, I looked up at the lifeguard to see if she noticed, but her head was turned the other way. Relieved, I continued to gasp for air, pretending my choking was nothing more than a persistent cough.

Finally, I finished one lap. Clutching the side of the pool with both arms, Jim joined me. "This (gasp) is much longer (gulp) than I thought," I sputtered, struggling to breathe.

"This is no dinky motel pool," Jim wheezed.

"But we begged her to let us swim (cough, cough), so we'd better swim, even if it kills us!" Our self-assured images of moments ago played like a cartoon. Yep, we're trim, we're fit, we're drowning!

That was thirteen years and thirty pounds ago; and although I'm no longer trim and fit, I still dive into waters for which I'm not conditioned. Spiritually, God strengthens us to face life's trials through prayer and Bible study. Independent, stubborn, and proud, I sometimes fool myself into thinking that I am strong enough to make it alone. But when the waters deepen and laps lengthen, I often drown in my circumstances. Luckily, the Lifeguard is watching, and God always jumps in to rescue me.

You'd think I would have learned by now that life's Olympic laps require God's conditioning. . .regardless of when the pool opens.

Target Heart Rate Scripture

"When you go through deep waters and great trouble, I will be with you. When you go through rivers of difficulty, you will not drown!" (Unless you decide to swim an Olympic lap!)

Isaiah 43:2 tlb

An Exercise in Laughter

LAUGHTER RELEASES STRESS. . . .

Pam and Beth's hectic schedules made it nearly impossible to schedule a day in which they could buy their mom a joint birthday gift, especially during the holidays. On their only day off, they met at the mall one afternoon to try to find the perfect gift. But everything that could go wrong did, and time was slipping away.

Frustrated and anxious, they pressed through the crowd; then, at the same moment, a store advertisement caught their eyes. It read: "ONE DAY ONLY. . . EVERYTHING OFF!"

"That's for sure!" both exclaimed aloud, thinking how "off" their one day had been. Instantly, they burst into laughter and their stress diminished.

Try this exercise:

When under pressure, take a deep breath and reassess your situation. Re-calling those serious-turned-humorous moments helps.

What works best for you when you are under stress? Share your stress busters in a group or with a friend to help one another get through a taxing time. Better yet, venture out on a shopping expedition!

Chapter 39
FORMAL DINING IN ROBES AND SLIPPERS

THE WARM-UP

Words a Woman Will Never Say: "You're so insensitive! How dare you consider dining out on our anniversary? You know how much more I'd rather stay home to roast a turkey, polish the silverware, and channel surf all evening!"

THE WORKOUT

Formal dinner parties present immediate problems for some of us. Since plowing through the meal without talking is rude, we feebly negotiate introductions with the strangers seated around our table. Next, we must ascertain the proper use of our tableware. *Which bread plate is mine? Is that my water glass on the right? Which fork and spoon do I use first, and for what?* Tensions rise as we wait for someone to make the first move so we can safely follow their lead and save ourselves from possible embarrassment. Of course, no one does; everyone just nods, smiles, sits erect with their hands in their laps, and talks about the weather.

So I've concluded that formal dinners are for looking good, not for eating. Think for a moment: It is uncouth to eat at a formal dinner, much less overeat. Eating comes much later, when one returns home and slips into one's all-you-can-eat-attire: a tattered robe and fuzzy slippers.

At one formal event I attended, I wore a white sequined suit and sat like a poised mannequin for at least twenty minutes before I broke under the pressure. Frankly, my growling stomach was talking louder than anyone in the room, so I decided to break the silence. I had no choice; everything I wanted was on the opposite end of the table.

"Excuse me," I asked the diamond-clad lady who sat across from me. "Would you please pass me the rolls and butter?"

I placed the roll and dab of butter on the bread plate, but it turned out that the plate belonged to someone else, which resulted in ruining everyone else's table setting. Embarrassed, I apologized as eight people rearranged their bread plates. What is it about formality that causes normal people to act stuffy and unapproachable?

In other areas of life we act in a similar way. Unsure of our place setting, we put on airs for fear of appearing foolish. Yet God accepts us just as we are, whether we are clad in diamonds or dressed down in denim. If anyone has reason to act stately and aloof, it's God, but He never does. Instead, He welcomes everyone to His banquet table, without reservations and without strict dress codes.

Having revealed my stupidity, I decided to forfeit any traces of etiquette and ask the big question: "Does anyone know which spoon is for what?"

"I was just wondering about that myself," the intellectual-looking man beside me responded, examining his place setting.

"Well, I know that the fat round one is for the soup," the diamond-clad lady chimed in.

Suddenly no one cared whose bread plate was whose or if the person seated next to him or her had used the proper eating utensil. In our hearts, tattered robes and fuzzy slippers had replaced the black ties and diamonds, and no one left hungry.

Good thing, because I was in an all-you-can-eat mood.

LAUGHTER THERAPY

TARGET HEART RATE SCRIPTURE

Jesus said: " 'I am the bread of life. He who comes to me will never go hungry, and he who believes in me will never be thirsty. . .and whoever comes to me I will never drive away.' " (Even dressed in tattered robes and slippers.)   JOHN 6:35, 37

Chapter 40
SECOND CHANCES AND CHOCOLATE CREAM PIE

THE WARM-UP

Words a Woman Will Never Say: "I tell you, Tricia has such incredible perception. Every time I see her she notices my weight gain, instructs me how to eat better, and reminds me when my roots need a touch-up. What would I do without a caring, insightful friend like her?"

THE WORKOUT

New treadmill? Check. Low-fat snacks? Check. Hand weights and exercise video? Check. All right, slip on those Nikes, and as the ad says, "Just do it!" Except. . . what about all of those holiday goodies?

My New Year's resolution to lose weight is nothing new. Each January I enter the process in preparatory stages. The first step? Eating my way through all the sweets left over from the holidays.

First the Christmas cookies and nut roll. Those are usually eliminated by New Year's Eve. Then the candies friends and relatives gave as gifts. I—with my husband's help—finished the box of Fannie May Pixies just in time for our neighbor to deliver a belated Christmas gift, a tin of Fannie May assortments inside a cute country basket. Yummy. How could I resist?

Again, Jim helped me eliminate those (he's so sacrificial). This freed me to polish off the container of hard candies I received just before Christmas. Hard candy lasts forever. . .except at our house.

But even after we purge our home of all those calories waiting to turn into body fat, I still have other hurdles to conquer. Namely, the second step: what to do at restaurants.

Fortified with willpower, I face the dining-out experience like a soldier girded for war. . .until I read the menu. My mind suggests, *Soup of the day and salad with low-fat vinaigrette,* but my mouth blurts out, "I'll have the fried chicken and fries." To ease my conscience, I request margarine instead of butter for the dinner rolls, and I order a diet soda. Who am I kidding?

Resolutions take commitment. Spiritually, it's much the same. Although God is a God of second chances, the first step comes when we recognize our sin and are willing to turn from it. Then, as we ask Christ to come into our lives and resolve to follow Him, He forgives us and gives us a new start.

But much like my battle of the bulge, some folks never press beyond the first step. Consequently, every year translates into a recurrent struggle with the same old temptations, the same problems.

As I thought about this, I considered something else. Dieting seldom works. We starve ourselves until we reach a desired weight, then swiftly return to our junk-food ways. But if we change our eating habits, healthy choices become a lifestyle and dieting is no longer necessary. In the same manner, committing our lives to Christ is a life-altering transformation of the heart that results in a brand-new lifestyle.

That's how I must view my attitude toward chocolate candy and mouthwatering desserts. So who knows, this could be the year I'll actually succeed.

I'd better get started. Let's see, lace up the Nikes. *Check.* Straddle the treadmill. *Check.* Turn the machine on and determine the settings. *Check.*

What? Who just came to the door? "Oh, hi, Neighbor. Thanks for the chocolate cream pie."

A new year, another day. Tomorrow; I'll think about all of this tomorrow.

TARGET HEART RATE SCRIPTURE

"Therefore, if anyone is in Christ, he is a new creation; the old has gone, the new has come!" (Along with the chocolate cream pie?)

2 CORINTHIANS 5:17

Chapter 41
NO MORE WEEDS IN THE LETTUCE SALAD

THE WARM-UP

Words a Woman Will Never Say: "Eating celery sticks and low-fat cottage cheese for the rest of my life is the ultimate thrill. But since I prefer the plus-size look, I guess I'll have to settle for peanut butter parfaits, fettuccini Alfredo, and double cheese sausage pizzas."

THE WORKOUT

There comes a day in every dieter's life when we'd prefer to toss our low-fat soups and salads into the sea of reckless abandon. I'm at that point now. After weeks of watching what I eat, I want to eat what I watch: whipped cream pies and foods that start with the letter "F", namely, fried chicken, French fries, and fried veggies served in one of those baskets lined in translucent paper where pools of grease puddle at the bottom.

But tipping the scale at an unmentionable weight has frightened me enough to load my grocery cart with low-fat cottage cheese, crunchy greens, yummy alfalfa sprouts, and soybean everything.

"I mean it, Jim," I announce with the earnestness of a reformed drug addict, "I refuse to eat 'that stuff' again."

"That stuff?"

"Yes, the junk food that turned this once-fit body into a life-size blob of Silly Putty."

Years ago, I was a health enthusiast. I jogged twenty-five miles a week, ate sensibly, and I kept the pounds off for years. Back then, I welcomed seeing people I hadn't talked to in years because I could flaunt my fit physique and bask in the flow of their compliments. Today, I duck behind boxes of Twinkies in the grocery store, hoping no one will notice me.

Of course, I have valid reasons for my weight gain. Here are a few favorites:

- Too little time and too tired to exercise consistently.

- Junk food is quicker and easier to make.

- Stress. (My mantra? When in stress, reach for a plate of double chocolate chip cookies.)

- Middle age. (I always hated the as-you-get-older-it's-harder-to-take-the-weight-off excuse. Now, unlike my clothing, it fits me well.)

Interestingly, my reasons for not doing what I know I should spill over into my spiritual life, too. Though my intentions are good, I allow daily intrusions to rob me from spending time with God. Read my Bible? Maybe later, after I finish my work. Quiet prayer time? I'm just too tired now; I need some sleep.

Excuses pop up faster than weeds after a summer rain. Sounds similar to a parable Jesus gave when He said that the kingdom of heaven was like a man who sowed good seed, but when everyone slept, the enemy sowed weeds among the wheat. The weeds of sin, worldly preoccupations, and lame excuses choke the seed of God's Word in our hearts. As a result, we become weakened, unproductive, and fruitless.

In moments of weakness, I have ignored the still small voice within. But not anymore.

"Yep, Jim, I'm staying with the program," I say, reinforcing my resolve. "No more excuses."

"What program?" my husband asks from somewhere in oblivion.

"You know, my *diet*?" I snarl. "No more weeds

among the lettuce salad for me!"

Confused, my husband exits. But I'm staying with the good seed of God's Word exclusively, even if that includes the alfalfa sprout variety.

TARGET HEART RATE SCRIPTURE

Jesus said, " 'The kingdom of heaven is like a man who sowed good seed. . . . But while everyone was sleeping, his enemy came and sowed weeds among the wheat. . . . When the wheat sprouted. . . , then the weeds also appeared.' " (But not for long; it's time to weed out the weeds.)

MATTHEW 13:24–26

Chapter 42
I'M WILLING, LORD; WHERE'S THE PASTRY BOARD?

THE WARM-UP

Words a Woman Will Never Say: "If I told you once, I've told you a thousand times—women's work is a snap. Maybe men assume women work hard because so little is expected of us."

THE WORKOUT

I view spending time in the kitchen like most men view a trip to the mall—get what you need and get out.

However, I came from a long line of women who spent most of their waking hours rolling dough, simmering soup, making stuffed cabbage, sausage, and much, much more. Women who would regard my lack of interest in the kitchen as a genetic defect of some sort. My mother is one of them. Mom is a pierogi-maker extraordinaire.

Pierogi, a triangular-shaped dumpling filled with potato-cheese mixture, plum butter, or sauerkraut, is a delicious ethnic dish and, more important, a family tradition. Mom makes pierogi as did her mother, as did her mother's mother.

Now Mom thinks it's time I learned how. "After all, I won't be around forever," she chided. "And you're not getting any younger, either."

Problem is, Mother's only daughter detests spending more than fifteen minutes in the kitchen at a time, and pierogi takes hours to make. But out of a sense of duty, I felt obliged to at least attempt to uphold the woman's role of culinary ethnicity in my ancestral line.

So Mom, in her time-to-do-some-serious-cooking apron, led me step by step. I did fine until I had to knead the dough. I lifted the gooey dough ball and plopped it down, giving it a hardy push as it hit Grandma's timeworn pastry board.

"No, no," Mom scolded. "Like this." She worked the dough in a graceful, rhythmic fashion.

Fold, press, lift, fold, press, lift. My turn. Somehow my press and lift was more like push and shove. My hands just wouldn't cooperate. I felt like a construction worker attempting to perform brain surgery while the head surgeon barked from behind, "You're killing the patient!"

But Mom graciously laughed instead, and I caught her shaking her head in disgust only two or three times when I did really stupid things.

We got through it, and with Mom's help, the pierogi were fit to eat. Most of all, I was assured that my Slovak grandma could now rest in peace.

Sometimes God, too, requires us to do things we would rather not do: Ask for forgiveness when we know we've been wrong. Forgive when we've been wronged. Give instead of take. Obey God's Word.

Though we resist, the Lord takes us through the process step by step. Our awkward attempts are frustrating; but if we will give it our best, God will overlook the really stupid things we do and work with us until the task is completed. After all, willingness is the first step to achievement.

I, however, have given up on becoming a pierogi connoisseur like my mother. Blame it on my genetic deficiency. Or could it be that I wasn't really willing to try in the first place?

On second thought, where's that pastry board? *I'm willing, Lord.*

TARGET HEART RATE SCRIPTURE

" 'If you are willing and obedient, you will eat the best from the land.' " (Eating the best in the land need not come from Mom's kitchen alone!)

ISAIAH 1:19

Chapter 43
MIRRORS

THE WARM-UP

Words a Woman Will Never Say: "If I'm unable to view this imperfect physique of mine from every angle, then I'm just not content. My goal is to face every flaw with thanksgiving and joy."

THE WORKOUT

Health clubs use a picture-is-worth-a-thousand-words philosophy. Their technique? Mirrors everywhere. From the locker room to the weight room, one cannot escape one's reflection. Whole walls are dedicated to revealing the truth of one's physical condition.

Recently, my son prodded me to visit a local health club with him. Since I've gained a few pounds (okay, more than a few), the idea of sweating and straining seemed reasonable.

My first session of step aerobics was a lesson in life. My son, who resembles the cover photo of a fitness magazine, escorted me to the aerobics room with its solid wall of floor-to-ceiling mirrors. Standing face-to-face with my bigger-than-life imperfect body was bad enough. But forced to compare my flaws with the long-legged leotard beauties who surrounded me was cruel. They appeared as if they indulged in step aerobics like I indulge in hot fudge sundaes. In a room flaunting Spandex and firm thighs, I stood out like a Jane Fonda reject in my baggy sweatpants and over-sized T-shirt. The twenty other people in the room needed a workout about as much as I needed another chocolate bonbon.

As the upbeat music blared, the instructor shouted, "March in place! Right foot step changes!" I concentrated intensely on following the lead of the svelte exercise enthusiast in front of me, who acted as if she had the lung capacity to run ten miles while humming the theme song to *Rocky*.

Forty minutes later, the mirrors revealed my true identity: Red-faced and clumsy, I stumbled to synchronize the step changes with the arm movements. As the session intensified, everyone counted aloud while shouting a vigorous *"Whoo!"* in sync to the beat of the music. Meanwhile, I stared at the face and body of a woman in desperate need of pulmonary resuscitation.

So I've concluded that mirrors accomplish one of two things: challenge us to realize our need to visit the health club more often—or humiliate the fatties among us, thereby eliminating baggy sweats from the premises completely.

The Bible works much the same way when the mirror of God's Word reflects our true image. The truth of who we are will either challenge us—or drive us away. We may accept the truth and ask God to change us, or we can ignore it and remain spiritually unfit.

At first we may feel embarrassed and clumsy; everyone will appear more conditioned as they flex their spiritual muscles. But God is a kind and patient instructor who welcomes those weighted down with sin. He sees us through to spiritual fitness. With God, baggy sweats transform into Spandex if we will only face our imperfect reflections.

Who knows? In time, we may even shout "Whoo!" with the best of them.

TARGET HEART RATE SCRIPTURE

"For whatever God says to us is full of living power. . .cutting swift and deep into our innermost thoughts and desires. . .exposing us for what we really are." (So bring on the mirrors. I'm ready for some spiritual conditioning!)

HEBREWS 4:12 TLB

Chapter 44

THE CLOTHESHORSE AND THE HORSE GONE TO PASTURE

THE WARM-UP

Words a Woman Will Never Say: "Please tell me the truth about my appearance; I'm longing to diminish my self-deception."

THE WORKOUT

My brother Marshall is a clotheshorse. And why not? He wears his clothes well. At fifty-something, he's physically fit and looks better than he ever has before. I only wish the same thing could be said for his seven-years-younger "little" sister.

One day his wife Jackie and I discussed the unfair advantage Marshall has over me. "That clotheshorse brother of mine really looks terrific," I commented in envy. After a pause I added, "But then you're a clotheshorse, too, Jackie."

"No, no," she protested. "Marshall owns a lot more clothes than I do and he wears them far better than I wear mine."

Yeah, sure, I thought inwardly. If Marshall is a clotheshorse, then Jackie is a clothes colt, and in my mind, that makes me a clotheshorse gone to pasture.

So what happened? My once burley, senior sibling has transformed into a suave sophisticate in his golden years. His flawless complexion and svelte physique give him the look of elegance, while my broad hips and touch of gray give me the look of a dumpling.

He boasts the best-dressed list like I boast how many oatmeal raisin cookies I can down in one sitting. Older brother's younger sister has slipped into middle age with the grace and finesse of a circus clown tumbling off a unicycle.

When Marshall and Jackie drive up from Missouri for a visit, my eldest brother's favorite pastime is clothes shopping. "No thanks," I tell him when he invites me along. "I'm waiting to lose weight before I buy any more clothes."

Whom am I kidding? The real reason for my shopping abstinence is that I refuse to buy one size larger. Instead, I squeeze into the smaller sized clothes that hang in my closet and convince myself that my inability to take deep breaths without splitting a zipper is merely a result of temporary bloating, nothing more.

In fact, I'm able to convince myself of just about anything. It's called self-deception. All one need do is ignore reality and opt for denial. Getting wider? Yes, but I still don't look that bad. Starting to sag? Maybe, but who isn't at my age? Need more exercise? I admit it, but how will I fit it into my busy schedule?

Spiritually, I do the same. Need to spend more time reading God's Word? Sure, but I've already memorized so much of the Bible. Getting spiritually drained? Maybe, but I still live a good Christian life. Before long my spiritual body sags in exhaustion from the harmful effects of daily living.

Perhaps the truth lies in the fact that my brother takes better care of himself than I do and that's why he wears his clothes well. He exercises, eats right, and gets adequate amounts of sleep.

Okay, no more self-deception. Like brother Marshall, I, too, have the ability to wear my clothes well. It's not a matter of aging poorly; it's a matter of getting and staying in condition despite one's age.

I may never be a clotheshorse, but at least I'll fit into my current wardrobe without turning blue. And that's a pretty good start for this old gray mare!

Target Heart Rate Scripture

"Let no man deceive himself." (And let no woman convince herself that temporary bloating has the power to split zippers.)

1 Corinthians 3:18 KJV

Chapter 45
RESTAURANTS AND WORKS OF ART

THE WARM-UP

Words a Woman Will Never Say: "Does it really matter where we eat? I realize the health department closed down that diner, but try to understand—all of my friends hang out there."

THE WORKOUT

My husband Jim and I love to frequent new restaurants. As we do, we review our built-in checklist. First, how's the food? Second, does it have a nonsmoking section well away from the smokers? Third, what's the atmosphere like? And finally, is it within our price range? Depending on our appetite, mood, or budget, any of the above is subject to change.

So for our anniversary we tried a new restaurant. Nonsmoking section? Yes. Ambiance? On the elegant side. Price? A bit extravagant, but it's a special occasion, so why not? Food? Well, let me put it this way. On a day when all we had to eat was a bowl of cereal, the food was. . .skimpy.

My entrée consisted of a single slice of roast beef with a tablespoon of gravy centered in the middle. Five carrots, sliced julienne style, were arranged diagonally around my microscopic piece of meat. Sprigs of parsley and other curly creations surrounded the brown and orange stuff.

The waiter, clad in starched white linen, placed the entrée in front of me, giving the plate a slight turn as he set it down. Why he turned it, I don't know. Since this was a ritzy place, I tried to appear dignified as I leaned toward my husband and commented, "Maybe turning the plate makes the carrots form a new pattern, similar to a kaleidoscope."

My husband glared at me with his I-can't-believe-you-said-that expression while the waiter served him. Meanwhile, I bit my upper lip, struggling to control the urge to break out in a chorus of "Is That All There Is?"

As we stared at our scant meals, the waiter boasted of the chef's ability to create "works of art." Politely, we smiled and nodded; but after he left, my husband leaned toward me and whispered, "With these prices, is it too much to ask for a little food with your plate? If we were looking for artistic expression, we would have visited the art museum."

"I guess we're just the type of people who prefer the

stick-to-your-ribs type of food where the vegetables, meat, and curly creations all touch each other," I replied.

Settling for the atmosphere, we resolved to stop grumbling and eat our meal, which took all of five minutes. Still hungry, we drank a lot of water and kept a close eye on the boy whose job was to circle the room dispensing one dinner roll at a time to hungry art lovers. "He's almost here," I assured my husband, who by now had ransacked the cracker basket for another saltine. Ambiance, we discovered, is a poor substitute for a hearty meal.

Similarly, some folks gravitate toward churches with ornate architecture, cushy pews, crystal chandeliers, and brass fixtures. Nothing wrong with that. But like our restaurant chef, the preacher serves his sermon as a work of art. He delivers his message with perfect annunciation, carefully arranged words, and flawless methodology. Yet for some of us, it lacks substance. We're looking for the kind of stick-to-your-ribs theology that sustains us long after we leave the church pew.

Perhaps for some the message isn't as important as the atmosphere in which it is served. But personally, I'd gladly forfeit other items on our spiritual checklist for one hearty portion of God's Word.

So we tried another restaurant recently. Nonsmoking section? Yes, a small one. Atmosphere? Homespun.

Price? Very reasonable. Food? Fantastic. Everything on our plates touched!

Target Heart Rate Scripture

" 'Blessed are those who hunger and thirst for righteousness, for they will be filled.' " (Without rations from the cracker basket or having to flag down the bread boy.)   MATTHEW 5:6

Chapter 46

BUOYANCY IS A WONDERFUL ASSET

THE WARM-UP

Words a Woman Will Never Say: "A day at the beach is an exhilarating event. Donned in my sleeveless muumuu, I sit on a beach blanket and wave to passersby while the ocean waves ripple in cadence with my flabby upper arms."

THE WORKOUT

Even in my slim-and-trim days, I stored enough body fat to bob like a cork whenever I touched water.

At first my buoyancy was a wonderful asset. Floating backside with arms and legs outstretched, I'd stare up at the summer sky as if reclined on a La-Z-Boy. Admiring my gift of levity, my husband and two sons watched in awe.

"Man, it's like Mom can float forever," son Jimmy observed. Afterward, I'd instruct the threesome on my floating techniques, but lacking adequate adipose to stay afloat for more than five seconds, each one sank the moment I released hold of them.

Soon, instead of admiration, I inspired vacation family fun. My buoyancy provided more laughter than a slapstick comedy as we routinely beelined for the hotel pool to devise water games.

"Let's toss a quarter to the bottom of the pool and see who gets it first," son Jeff suggested. As we plunged into the water, Dad and boys sank with brick consistency, while I struggled to lunge deep enough to reach the bottom of the pool. Hysterical with laughter, my husband shot to the surface to grab my arm and pull me down, providing leverage. Meanwhile, the kids paddled to the bottom, leaving behind a stream of bubbles from their underwater guffaws.

Nevertheless, I boasted one award-winning game: Who could tread water the longest? "Hey, that's no fair!" Jimmy protested at the mere mention of the game as his brother Jeff chimed in. "Yeah, we all know Mom is unsinkable!"

After the jesting subsided, my husband, the voice of sensitivity and compassion, soothed me with his trademark brand of consolation. "Look on the positive side, Honey," he said, concealing a grin. "Your built-in life preserver might come in handy someday. I mean, think of how many people you could have saved on the *Titanic*."

I leveled a stern scowl in his direction. "Yeah, that's right, just throw my body overboard and instruct people to latch on!"

Perhaps my heartless husband had a point, though. God views us much differently than we view ourselves; He sees the possibilities beneath our flaws. Our imperfections serve as steppingstones for God to work in our lives. Rather than dwelling on the negatives, the Lord maximizes our lives to their fullest potential, despite our apparent flaws.

With that in mind, I choose to consider my buoyancy as a positive trait. After all, for a woman who fears scales more than she fears the dentist's drill, treading water is the only time I actually experience weightlessness. No matter how much body fat accumulates, I'm a featherweight in water, and life is smooth sailing. . .I mean, floating.

And hey, let's not underestimate my unique life-saving capabilities!

TARGET HEART RATE SCRIPTURE

"Does not the potter [God] have the right to make out of the same lump of clay some pottery for noble purposes and some for common use?" (And some for floating and some for sinking?)

ROMANS 9:21

Chapter 47
PALE LEGS SPRINGTIME STRUGGLE

THE WARM-UP

Words a Woman Will Never Say: "All right. I apologize for flaunting my dimpled thighs. But I thought their craterlike formations were really artistic, and before I knew it, pride got the best of me."

THE WORKOUT

Each spring, more than daylilies and daffodils burst from winter's darkness. Pale legs, shaded from the summer sun, also appear at the first balmy rise in temperature. Some pop out, others plop, but they surface just the same.

For the ploppers among us, this is spring's first struggle—a time when we refuse to wear shorts as a matter of dignity. Colorless legs are bad enough, but ones that resemble dimpled elephant stumps are enough to cause some of us to pray for an arctic blast in mid-June.

So in late spring I join those who laboriously

catch the rays to tan their shapeless lard-laden legs. A bronze tone compensates for the lack of firm, been-sweating-in-the-gym-all-winter thighs, I reason. But experience reminds me that bumpy cellulite comes in all colors. You can tan it, tone it, slip nylons over it to hold it together, but short of liposuction, it's a lost cause.

I am preoccupied with camouflaging human flaws, nonetheless. I apply makeup and creams to contour my face, conceal wrinkles, and firm droopy eyelids tauter than a soldier's army bunk. Oversized shirts hide my midsection, and baggy jeans lose heavy hips in a sea of denim.

Eventually, however, the camouflage is removed. The Maybelline is washed off at the end of the day, and unshed pounds make their seasonal debut in the summer's sun. As the adage goes, "You can run, but you can't hide." At least not for long.

But I try anyway, even with more "weighty" matters than physical flaws. I often try to conceal poor attitudes and bad habits with spiritual clichés and Sunday smiles, but sooner or later the summer sunshine of God's Holy Word exposes my spiritual lumps and jiggles.

Spring's first struggle is often undignified. . .but it's necessary. We may deny it, cover it, or boast our Sunday best and act like it isn't there, but sooner or later our spiritual imperfections surface.

However, there is hope: When our flaws meet the Son, Christ promises to forgive, heal, firm, and reshape our lives so that we'll never have to hide again.

So whisk out the shorts and struggle no more. It's springtime!

TARGET HEART RATE SCRIPTURE

"Can any hide himself in secret places that I [God] shall not see him?" *(No, Lord, not even beneath baggy sweats and oversized shirts; but would You mind not shining so brightly upon my pale, lard-laden legs?)*   JEREMIAH 23:24 KJV

An Exercise in Laughter
LAUGHTER WARMS THE SOUL. . . .

A lighthearted story. . .a smile from your toddler after a long day of frowns. . .a humorous card from an old friend received when you need it most. . .

These all warm the soul better than hot tea served in one of Grandmother's delicate china cups. Often our weary souls need gentle hugs given in simple yet meaningful ways.

One instance happened to me. I had owned my brand-new car for a brief two weeks when I had a fender bender one evening. My then four-year-old grandson Ian was with my husband when I arrived home. Visibly shaken, I fought back the tears that trickled down my cheeks as I explained what happened. Before my husband could respond, Ian jumped to his feet and locked his arms around my neck. "Don't worry, Nana, I forgive you for bonking your car." Tears turned to smiles as the three of us embraced with heartwarming hugs.

Anxiety, depression, or sadness freezes the soul in winter's blast of despair. But laughter breaks the ice. The ability to laugh despite our circumstances warms the soul and melts the heart.

Try this exercise:

Recall a time when the loving gesture of a child, family member, or friend melted your chill of despair. Then extend a similar gesture to someone you know. Mail a humorous card and include a heartwarming note.

Do it today.

Chapter 48
HIDE THE TAFFY!

THE WARM-UP

Words a Woman Will Never Say: "Barbara said she was willing to give herself all the credit for the work I did on the church banquet. I told her I would assume credit if she preferred, but she insisted on giving it all to herself. I tell you, she exemplifies the essence of humility. I appreciate her attitude so much."

THE WORKOUT

I recall the recurring temptation on several family vacations to the Smoky Mountains, home of a candy store that made saltwater taffy on the premises. Passersby viewed the procedure through a glass window as machines pulled and twisted the gooey confectionery to mouthwatering delectability. Much as a dog drools for a bone, I salivated all of five minutes before entering the store to buy a box.

Before we returned to our cabin, I managed to wolf down a number of taffy rolls. And every time, my awareness of the compulsion plagued me. What in the world was I doing? Turning to the kids, I shoved the box in their hands as if playing a game of hot potato. As empty wrappers drifted to the floor, I'd say in my most commanding voice: "Hide this where I can't find it, Guys."

As if on cue, my two masterful sons would devise a plan. They'd instruct me to close my eyes as they'd embark on another hide-the-taffy-from-Mom adventure. A few minutes would pass. "You'll never find it, Mom; we hid it really well this time!" they'd announce with boastful grins.

Seems they underestimated my candy cravings. For a while, I'd be fine. Maybe even for a whole day. Then as soon as my family trekked poolside, I'd lag behind searching for "the box." *Just one,* I'd rationalize, checking underneath the bed, inside the cabinets, and between the linens, until. . .aha! Found it.

"What we need is a kitchen safe with a lock and key!" my family would tease when they returned to find me chomping on a wad of strawberry twirl.

I wonder how different our lives would be if we would search for God with unrestrained craving instead of the things that don't matter? Some crave success; others covet wealth, possessions, or personal acclaim. But how many of us crave a deeper walk with God above all else? Do we gaze through the window of His Word, desiring to become what He wants us to be, to do whatever He instructs, and know Him more intimately?

Imagine handing the Bible to our children, saying, "Hide this. I'm reading too much of it!" And then, because our love for God is so strong, we'd uncover every nook and cranny to satisfy our desire to draw closer to Him.

When God becomes our primary focus, we have little need for wealth, fame, or kitchen vaults because He will be our greatest desire. And who knows, maybe even saltwater taffy would lose its allure, even with my nose pressed against a candy store window.

Target Heart Rate Scripture

"But seek ye first the kingdom of God, and his righteousness; and all these things shall be added unto you." (Minus the saltwater taffy.)

MATTHEW 6:33 KJV

Chapter 49
THEY STILL FIT—OR THEY'RE TOO TIGHT

THE WARM-UP

Words a Woman Will Never Say: "If a picture is worth a thousand words, I'm staring at a masterpiece. This photo makes me look as heavy as I really am. I love accuracy."

THE WORKOUT

For those of us past forty, an exhilarating phrase is voiced in jubilation when we retrieve last year's blue jeans, zip them up, and can honestly say, "They still fit." Those three little words take on a whole new meaning in middle age.

No uncomfortable snugness. No tug-of-war with the zipper. No waistband that curls under a roll of flab or a button that digs into layers of lard. What could be sweeter than that? It's enough to reward oneself with a Dove ice cream bar and a bag of Cheetos.

Unfortunately, on New Year's Day, I choked out three very different words instead: "They're too tight." The irony of it all is that last year my husband and I went on a weight-loss program. In four months I lost fourteen pounds of fat and increased my muscle mass, all without thrusting myself into martyrdom while nibbling on scraps of lettuce and dry rice cakes. So how did I land on the high end of the scale a year later?

Blame it on stress, or not enough time to eat properly and exercise, or. . . Truth is, I suffer from a discipline deficit when it comes to food. We all have our weaknesses, and French fries are mine. So is candy, and did I mention homemade cookies? Especially the chewy kind. Yum.

After the holidays, I tried to ignore the fact that my clothes were shrinking again. "I've got to remember to adjust the settings on the washer and dryer," I told myself.

Then I went to the doctor for my annual exam. Women hate those checkups, but what I detest most is stepping on the scale before the exam. In comparison, everything else is a cakewalk. (There I go thinking in terms of food again.)

"Oh boy, you gained twelve pounds since your last visit," the female doctor announced when she entered the examining room, unaware that I instructed her nurse to *not tell me my weight* when, with clenched eyelids, I stepped on the scale. So the fat, I mean the cat, was out of the bag, and my days of denial were over.

For years I whisked through life hooked on overindulgence. I appeared unscathed, until the junk food caught up with my body. But change is possible. All I need do is confront my shortcomings. The doctor's visit exposed mine. . .well, okay, one of mine. Since then I've concentrated less on squeezing into my jeans and more on fitting exercise and proper nutrition into my life. Not only for appearance sake, but because I'd like to live a long and healthy life so I can enjoy my family and watch my grandchildren grow up.

After all, "I love you" are the only three words sweeter than "They still fit." Well, maybe there are just three more: "They're too loose!"

TARGET HEART RATE SCRIPTURE

Jesus said, "For there is nothing covered, that shall not be revealed; neither hid, that shall not be known." (Neither eaten that shall not eventually show up around the thighs and hips.)

LUKE 12:2 KJV

Chapter 50
KITCHEN DUTY

THE WARM-UP

Words a Woman Will Never Say: "No, no please, allow me to clean up the dinner dishes. Other than cooking all your meals, laundering your clothes, running your errands, and raising your children, I seldom do anything just for you. So kick back, relax, and watch the sports channel all day."

THE WORKOUT

Years ago when we first talked about building a new home, my husband and I tried to determine the things we really needed and the things we could live without.

"I know one way to cut costs," Jim quipped. "Omit the kitchen. We don't use the one we have now."

That was my cue to laugh. I didn't, but he continued. "Yep, all we'll have to do is set a cooler in the bedroom just in case we want a cold soda or something."

I admit it. The kitchen is not my forte. When our sons were young, I cooked every day. Now that they're grown, I feel I've served my time in the family mess hall. In fact, a transfer to a different unit would thrill me, or at least a promotion from the galley to above-deck duties.

Unlike men, women are expected to cook and clean. I realize this practice dates back to biblical times, but must I enjoy it? However, I've noticed the younger generation rejects the you-woman-you-cook concept.

When a relative visited us from out of town, we gathered at Mom and Dad's for a family dinner: my husband and I, son Jim and his bride Robin, son Jeff and his wife Theresa, and our twenty-four-year-old cousin—a total of five women. Mom, who gladly accepts kitchen duty as her lot in life, served a huge meal, as is her custom. Afterward, the men did what they do best—migrated to the family room to watch television while the women cleared the table. Mom jumped up (she barely sat down through dinner) and forged into the kitchen, balancing plates and bowls in both hands. I helped, while the younger women dispersed in the same direction as the men.

"Ah–mm–ahem," I stammered, as they meandered away. "Come on, Girls. Everyone helps."

Theresa joined the galley slaves willingly, while I pulled daughter Robin by the hand toward the mess hall. Jamie must have thought the dinner was in her honor so she could abstain. "You, too, Cousin Jamie," I coaxed.

I was now deemed a tyrant. "I don't see why the men don't help, too," daughter Robin argued. *Good point,* I thought. Suddenly my feminism surfaced.

"Yeah, why is it that women spend hours cooking only to spend more time cleaning up everyone's mess?" I grumbled.

"You know what my mother always said," Dad chimed in from his seat of comfort. "If you ate, you help clean up!"

Was my imagination running away with me? I could have sworn Dad ate, too. But what's the point? "Right, Dad," I said in resignation as I continued to work.

In the Old Testament, Samuel warned the people what would happen if they insisted on having a king rule them. "He will take your daughters from you and force them to cook and bake," he said. Note the word "force." That's exactly how I feel in the kitchen. Seems a few Old Testament ladies felt the same way.

So here's how I view it. Although a man is king of his castle, he should still clean up the mess he helped to make. Either that, or hand me a cooler. From now on, I'm using the mess hall for above-deck activities only. I've been promoted.

TARGET HEART RATE SCRIPTURE

"They broke bread in their homes and ate together with glad and sincere hearts." (And afterward, the women forged below deck, while the men resumed their kingly thrones.)

ACTS 2:46

Chapter 51
FOR ALL YOU SUGAR JUNKIES

THE WARM-UP

Words a Woman Will Never Say: "Don't tell me I need more sweets in my diet. I'm aware of that and I'm trying my best to eat more. Just give me time. It takes discipline to achieve such a lofty goal."

THE WORKOUT

I've noticed something interesting about myself. The only solicitors I welcome to my door are schoolchildren toting cardboard boxes filled with candy.

Now why is that? Is it because I'm sympathetic toward the little darlings? Ah, no. Is it because I'm a mother and understand the importance of fund-raising? Afraid not. Rather, my benevolence stems from something more self-indulgent, namely, my sweetaholic tendencies.

That's right, I admit it. I relish the instant gratification I receive whenever one of those giant-size chocolate candy bars appeases my sugar cravings. What's more, I like it even better when obtaining my fix takes little or no effort on my part.

But I'm not alone. At the office I've seen entire boxes of candy wiped out in a matter of hours. In fact, one way to increase your child's candy sales is to take a full box with you to your place of employment. It's a sure sell.

Gift wrap, candles, and all-occasion cards don't have the same persuasive marketing capabilities that candy does. Why? Because sweetaholics are in the majority, and we will do just about anything to satisfy our cravings.

One sure sign of a sugar junkie is her willingness to buy. Most times, it is unnecessary to approach a sweetaholic to make a sale. We're the ones who exclaim, "Oh good! You still have a few peanut butter cups left!" as we cheerfully dish out another two dollars before the person holding the box of candy can so much as open his or her little mouth.

What's the big attraction anyway? Candy is junk. It's loaded with empty calories and has zero nutritional value; yet our uncontrollable cravings for it drive us to obsessive behavior.

Yesterday a student came to my door selling candy for a school fund-raiser. I was thrilled. I bolted up the stairs to search for money while the schoolgirl stood outside my door. The inside of my purse looked like a war zone as I frantically scrambled through it for signs of loose change. Gathering a handful of coins, I dashed downstairs, eager to pay the child, grab the candy, and head for the nearest chair to savor my M&Ms.

That's when it occurred to me: When was the last time I bolted up the stairs, grabbed my Bible, and headed for the nearest chair to savor the food of God's Word?

The Bible tells us to "Taste and see that the LORD is good" (Psalm 34:8). That first "taste" comes when we choose to feast at the table of God's Word; unlike the junk food of life, Jesus satisfies. The Bible is the spiritual food by which we grow; it contains the life-sustaining meat and potatoes we all require. It is packed with nutrients that provide salvation for our souls, strength for our spirits, renewal for our minds, and hope for our futures. To those who ingest its life-giving words, the Scriptures provide strength and restoration. So why do I opt for the junk foods of life instead?

Oops, excuse me a minute, someone else is at my door. "You're selling chocolate what? Ah, no thanks. I'm a meat-and-potato person myself."

TARGET HEART RATE SCRIPTURE

" 'Blessed are those who hunger and thirst for righteousness, for they will be filled.' " (And never crave junk food again.)

MATTHEW 5:6

Chapter 52
BLUEBERRY SMILE

THE WARM-UP

Words a Woman Will Never Say: "Talking on the telephone is like holding my breath underwater. I pretend to listen and, after a few minutes of forced silence, I gasp for air and plunge into nonstop chatter. It's one of the traits my husband loves most about me."

THE WORKOUT

During our first visit to Hawaii, we took Angela, my brother George's then six-year-old granddaughter, out for breakfast before church. I had just finished devouring blueberry pancakes smothered in copious amounts of fresh blueberries and syrup of the same.

For no apparent reason, Angela began to giggle. Covering the tee-hees with her hand, she stared up at me, but I kept talking. Then my husband dissolved into laughter.

"All right. What's so funny?" I said, waiting for a jokester response.

"Your. . .your teeth," Angela snickered.

"What?"

"Your teeth are blue!" my husband rasped through growing guffaws, his squinted eyes wet with tears.

We were due to meet my brother George and his wife Lena at their church in fifteen minutes. Ordinarily that wouldn't be a problem. Except George had anticipated and talked about our arrival for months, bragging about his "sister the newspaper columnist" to the pastor and church family within the tiny congregation.

"Everyone is excited about meeting you on Sunday," George had said eagerly, the moment we landed on Maui. I felt like a movie star, or a statesman, or someone equally undeserving.

So there I was with my blueberry smile, yet another image to uphold, and no toothbrush in sight. I feverishly picked up a paper napkin, wrapped the tip of my finger, and dipped it into the water glass. Rubbing hard, I worked the wet napkin back and forth across my teeth as visions of first introductions thrust me into a panic. "Just don't smile," my husband offered between guffaws, still dabbing the tears from his eyes.

What I had just put inside had left its mark on the outside, and I could do little to remove the evidence. My smile, or lack of it, would give me away.

The face is the one part of our body that reveals

more than we think. Other parts are easy to conceal. For instance, an oversized T-shirt conceals spare tires around the midsection, and we can conveniently squeeze bad hair under a hat. But one glance at the face reveals much of what is going on inside the person. In my case that Sunday morning, gluttony.

As a parent, I can read my sons' faces. With one glance I detect fatigue, frustration, confusion, anger, joy, even sin. Their expressions—a smirk, an eye movement, a frown, or a raised eyebrow—say more than the words they speak. We may think we can fool folks into believing that all is well, but the countenance tells all, revealing the stains of the heart or, in my case, the stains of the teeth.

The teeth scrubbing removed some of the blueberry stains so that by the time we arrived at church, my once-pearly-whites-stained-blue had brightened to an ashen gray. As George introduced his "sister the newspaper columnist," I smiled faintly, exposing myself for the blueberry glutton I am, thereby deflating the celebrity status I could have enjoyed.

But at least I had one conciliation—the loose-fitting dress I wore concealed the really significant flaws!

LAUGHTER THERAPY

Target Heart Rate Scripture

"The look on their faces testifies against them."
(So do the stains on her teeth.)

ISAIAH 3:9

Chapter 53
DISCIPLINED, ANNOYING PEOPLE

THE WARM-UP

Words a Woman Will Never Say: "The twelve pounds I gained on vacation make all the difference. I no longer slip into my clothes. Nope, everything I wear is tugged or pulled on with loud, satisfying grunts. My clothes feel tight, and I feel great."

THE WORKOUT

I once knew two delightful, yet overly disciplined people who annoyed me more than being stalled in traffic with two hungry, whiney kids clamoring in the backseat.

Even on Saturdays, Beth and Robert awakened at 7 A.M., eager to begin their daily routine. It went something like this: forty-five minutes of exercise followed by a fifteen-minute shower and a leisurely breakfast to begin their day. They ate the same high-fiber, low-calorie meal each morning—a bowl of oat bran, a slice of dry wheat toast, a half glass of orange juice, and one cup of decaffeinated coffee. Black.

I once commented on their strict regimen, and Beth told me they really weren't that stringent. "On our off days we treat ourselves to an occasional sprinkle of wheat germ and sip of aloe vera juice," she insisted.

Their nine-hour workdays began as they sailed out the door whistling, "Oh what a beautiful morning. . . ." After an exhilarating day's work, they returned home to prepare their low-fat, low-cholesterol dinner of broiled fish (no oil), baked potato (minus butter), and hearty portions of green vegetables (without butter). Following their nutritious meal, they enjoyed one full hour of spontaneous leisure time, followed by an hour of devotions, and thirty minutes of network news before retiring.

Without fail, Beth and Robert's structured lifestyle often magnified my lack thereof. One day, as my husband and I discussed our shortcomings, we realized we had slipped in the area of self-discipline over the years. "We weren't always like this," I said, rationalizing.

"I know," my husband answered. "We ate right, made quality time for the Lord, and jogged four to seven miles each day."

"I wonder what happened?" I asked, as I reached inside the freezer for the carton of chocolate swirl ice cream. "I'm so out of shape, I'm embarrassed to jog in shorts. With each heel strike, my thighs jiggle like Jell-O."

Jim laughed. I didn't, so he changed the subject. "And remember how much time we spent in Bible study?"

"Don't remind me," I said, slurping a spoonful, "I feel guilty enough."

Whenever I do what I know I shouldn't, I become discontented and depressed. Maybe that's why the Bible encourages us to lead a disciplined life. Discipline is freedom, because it frees us from the bondage of excessive, compulsive behavior that results in sin.

Later, my husband came up with a solution. He calls it our "walk and talk time."

Each morning from 6 to 7:30 A.M., he plans to exercise while he prays at the same time.

"Do you want to join me?" he asked enthusiastically.

"Too early," I replied. "I think I'll begin my walk and talk time closer to eight."

So today was Jim's first day of implementing his program. Today was mine, too. Not great, but better than I expected. Although I think I need help. Self-discipline apart from God's assistance is like riding in a horse-drawn wagon without the horse.

But the first step to a disciplined life is, at least, a

beginning. Meanwhile. . .pass the butter. Well, maybe just a dab.

TARGET HEART RATE SCRIPTURE

"I don't understand myself at all, for I really want to do what is right, but I can't. I do what I don't want to—what I hate." (So please help, Lord. Only promise You'll stop short of having me whistle "Oh What a Beautiful Morning.")

ROMANS 7:15 TLB

Chapter 54
DO I LOOK THE PART?

THE WARM-UP

Words a Woman Will Never Say: "Ziplock bags and plastic storage containers? Not me, Sister. I refuse to subject my family to leftovers."

THE WORKOUT

Legs crossed and one arm resting on the back of the bench, Jim made himself comfortable outside the store while I shopped. The mall is the perfect place for people watchers. Years of benchwarming has made my husband a master spectator.

But this time the tables were turned. Unbeknownst to Jim, a young couple had been observing him for some time. Finally, the teen approached him.

"You're an undercover cop, aren't you?" the young man asked as his humiliated girlfriend tugged at his sleeve to pull him away.

"No," Jim said with a faint smile, "I'm not."

"Liar," the teen said crisply and walked away.

Oddly, the incident tickled Jim, because all his life he's dreamed of becoming a private detective.

"Hey, Jim," I said, after hearing what happened. "That's a compliment! At least you look the part."

That got me thinking. My imagination dipped and twirled as I mused about my own secret fantasy—to become a professional figure skater. Suddenly, I envisioned someone approaching me, declaring with confidence, "You're a world-class ice skater, aren't you?!"

With grace and humility, I'd deny it, yet they would refuse to believe I wasn't Nancy Kerrigan or Katarina Witt.

As my fantasy continued, my self-image catapulted toward the sky while I bubbled with ego-boosting effervescence. Elated, I performed a triple toe loop into the nearest sports store (I'm envisioning hard here). As other fans pressed to ask for my autograph, I purchased my first pair of skates and a sequined bodysuit to accentuate my svelte physique (Okay, I'm really stretching now).

The way I see it, looking the part is the first step to being the real thing. After all, that's what we're told before we go on a job interview. Look and think success, and you'll be successful. Or how about weight control? Envision yourself thin and presto! The pounds shed like dog hair.

Believing is important; however, the Book of James tells us "faith without works is dead." It's not enough to imagine being successful, or thin, or even living the Christian life. We must, at some point, take the necessary steps to implement our good intentions. Appearances are deceptive. We can fool some people, but we can't fool God. Making the effort is what matters.

Though he looks the part and undoubtedly visualizes leading a covert reconnaissance mission, Jim is no undercover cop except, perhaps, in his wildest imagination and in the confused mind of a cocky teenager. But then, I'm no figure skater, either. Although I must admit, I would love it if someone actually thought I was.

Hmm, maybe next time I should warm the bench while Jim shops. Who knows, that young couple might pass by again and mistake me for an Olympic gold medalist. Or perhaps, at the very least, an aspiring ice skater. Or. . .ah, maybe a middle-aged wannabe? Or they might just walk on by.

So much for looking the part.

TARGET HEART RATE SCRIPTURE

"As he thinketh in his heart, so is he."(Unless the man or woman thinks he or she is a private detective or an Olympic ice-skating champion.)

PROVERBS 23:7 KJV

An Exercise in Laughter

LAUGHTER HEALS THE PAIN. . . .

The late Norman Cousins, author of *Anatomy of an Illness,* was an advocate for the health benefits of humor. As a sufferer of ankylosing spondylitis—a disease that afflicts the joints between the spinal vertebrae— Cousins discovered that ten minutes of belly laughter gave him two hours of pain-free, drug-free sleep.

After the 1964 diagnosis of his disease (for which there was no cure), Cousins realized that massive doses of medication were toxic. So he decided to try laughter instead. At home he spent hours watching Marx Brothers films and reading humorous stories. Within days he was off all painkillers and sleeping pills. Later, he wrote an article in the *New England Journal of Medicine* about his findings, but he was sorely criticized.

Finally, on January 27, 1989, the *Journal of the American Medical Association* published an article giving Cousins's claims credibility. In an article entitled,

"Laugh If This Is a Joke," Lars Ljungdahl, a Swedish researcher, concluded that "a humor therapy program can increase the quality of life for patients with chronic problems. . .laughter has an immediate symptom-relieving effect for these patients. . . ."

God knew that all along; that's why He promised, "A merry heart doeth good like a medicine" (Proverbs 17:22 KJV). When physical or mental pain torments the mind and body, laughter suppresses stress, relaxes tension, and kills the pain.

Try this exercise:

Do you know someone who is ill and needs cheering up? Plan a visit or a lunch date and bring along a humorous book, a funny story, or a comedy video to share. Use the previous story to inspire and motivate. More important, laugh often and smile always!

Inspirational Library

Beautiful purse/pocket-size editions of Christian classics bound in flexible leatherette. These books make thoughtful gifts for everyone on your list, including yourself!

When I'm on My Knees   The highly popular collection of devotional thoughts on prayer, especially for women.
Flexible Leatherette $4.97

The Bible Promise Book   Over 1,000 promises from God's Word arranged by topic. What does God promise about matters like: Anger, Illness, Jealousy, Love, Money, Old Age, and Mercy? Find out in this book!
Flexible Leatherette $3.97

Daily Wisdom for Women   A daily devotional for women seeking biblical wisdom to apply to their lives. Scripture taken from the New American Standard Version of the Bible.
Flexible Leatherette $4.97

My Daily Prayer Journal   Each page is dated and features a Scripture verse and ample room for you to record your thoughts, prayers, and praises. One page for each day of the year.
Flexible Leatherette $4.97

Available wherever books are sold.
Or order from:

Barbour Publishing, Inc.
P.O. Box 719
Uhrichsville, OH 44683
http://www.barbourbooks.com

If you order by mail, add $2.00 to your order for shipping.
Prices are subject to change without notice.